FINANCIAL CHEAT CODES

FINANCIAL CHEAT CODES

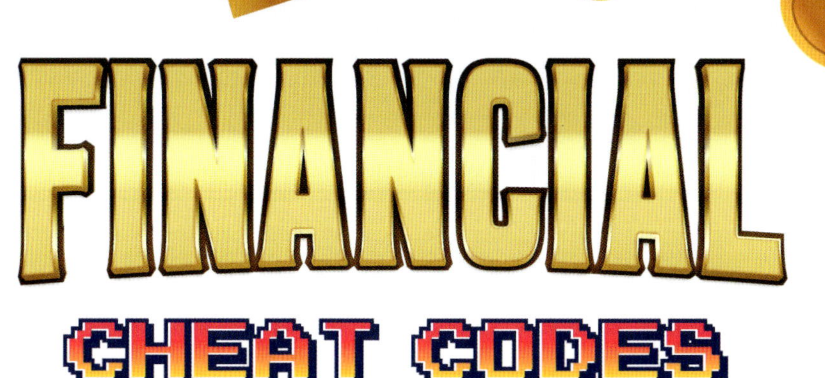

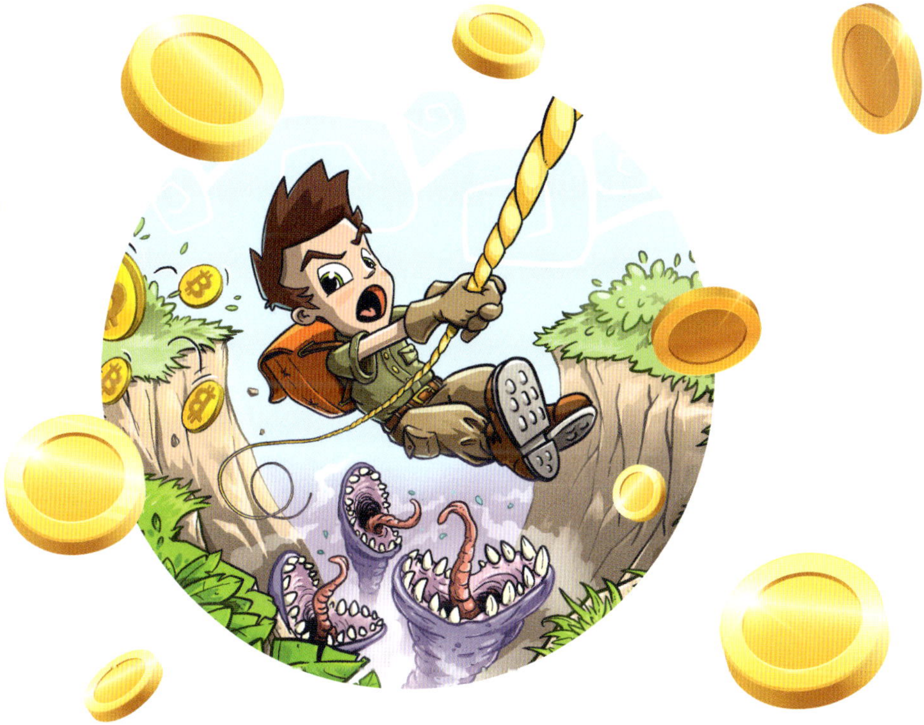

HOW TO WIN THE GAME OF FINANCE

SEAN DEMPSEY

Peter E. Randall Publisher
Portsmouth, New Hampshire
2026

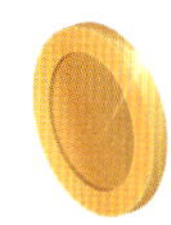

Disclaimer

The information contained in this book is provided for educational and informational purposes only and should not be construed as financial, investment, legal, or tax advice. No part of this publication constitutes a solicitation, offer, or recommendation to buy or sell any security, real estate, or other financial instrument, or to participate in any investment strategy.

The author and publisher make no representations, warranties, or guarantees as to the accuracy or completeness of the information presented, and expressly disclaim any liability for errors or omissions. Readers are encouraged to perform their own due diligence and consult with qualified financial, legal, and tax professionals before making any investment decisions.

Past performance is not indicative of future results. All investments involve risk, including the possible loss of principal. The reader assumes full responsibility for any actions taken based on the contents of this book.

Copyright and Trademark Notice

The extremely brief *Mario 3* gameplay depictions (as retold from my childhood in the Preface) was done with the full knowing and understanding that the named video game and any/all descriptions of its gameplay remain the exclusive property of its original creators and are fully owned and copyrighted by *Nintendo* and its subsidiaries.

Any likeness to any proprietary or trademarked character(s) mentioned or shown in this book is completely accidental.

ISBN: 978-1-942155-89-8
Library of Congress Control No.: 2025922592

Published by
Peter E. Randall Publisher
5 Greenleaf Woods Drive #102
Portsmouth, NH 03801
http://www.perpublisher.com

Printed in the United States of America

DEDICATION

This book is dedicated to my lovely wife who continues to push me daily to be a better version of myself—a better husband, a better father, and a better man.

May I one day evolve into the stellar person I have somehow fooled her into thinking I am.

A wise man leaves an inheritance for his children's children.
Proverbs 13:22

TABLE OF CONTENTS

FOREWORD

Because I am a self-proclaimed "Recovering CPA" and a Certified Infinite Banking Concept Practitioner, people who want to be in control of their finances and their future ask me where to start. If you are reading the book, you have found the answer.

I have worked with Sean over the years to incorporate Infinite Banking into his life and have interviewed him multiple times on the Infinite Wealth Podcast. Each time I speak with Sean, I feel like I learned something of value. One of the things I like about this book and Sean is that he is talking from experience. Or as Robert Kiyosaki would say, a "real teacher." Not only has Sean implemented the tactics in this book himself, but they can also be implemented by anyone willing to put in this effort.

There are great books out there. Many are referred to in this book. However, this book is the place to start. This is your "cheat code" to allow you to achieve your goals, aka win the game, in less time with less effort. The other books focus on one topic, i.e., Infinite Banking, Real Estate, paying less in taxes. However, this book provides the foundation on the crucial topics you need to understand on how to win the game of finance. By having that foundation, you can accelerate your learning as you dive deeper into each topic.

This is only the beginning of your path to living the life you want. This book is the best place to start your journey.

I wish you success in winning your financial game,

Anthony J. Fazo CPA

Host of *The Infinite Wealth Podcast*

WARP FOUND!

PREFACE

You may be asking yourself: "*So, what's with the book title?*"

"*What the hell is a 'Financial Cheat Code'?*"

Well, inquisitive reader, I'll tell you!

Being a child of the 80s, I naturally played my fair share of 2D video games. The ones that consumed most of my early childhood were the Super Mario Brothers on the NES Gaming System (that's "The Original Nintendo" to you youngsters).

As some may recall, these life-changing games were played with little, gray, **wired,** rectangular controllers on your basement's 24" tube television set. **The good ol' days!**

Specifically, "**Mario 3**" completely captivated me with its insidious gameplay, **killer** graphics (at the time they were quite novel), and enigmatic features (e.g., it had both a "raccoon tail" that let you briefly fly, as well as a "frog suit" to let you swim, etc.).

In short, it was THE BEST! It was *the* game all the kids were playing. It was a cultural zeitgeist.

Buried deep within–*hidden*–were these little "cheats" called "*Warp Whistles*" that allowed you to essentially SKIP from the level you were on to distant levels you wouldn't get to until much later in the game. *(Because it's only natural that playing a magical yellow lute ports you to another world.)*

But here's the point: these weren't just "nice to find" items–they were *essential* if you wanted to have a shot at beating the game!

Finding the *Warp Whistles* early on gave you a *massive* advantage. It was a total game-changer!

When you're seven or eight years old, you aren't interested in "enjoying every level." There wasn't an intrinsic joy in delaying and solving each puzzle and every world of gameplay. The GOAL was to *finish* the game and take every possible shortcut you could along the way!

Not to mention, those little analog NES cartridges that contained the programming were finnicky. The slightest bump—heck, even a strong *sneeze*—would completely freeze the console or restart it! All your hours of progress were lost! When that happened, you had to lugubriously walk over to the NES box, take the cartridge out, and then BLOW, BLOW, BLOW into the bottom of it. And then put it back in.

Whoops, that didn't work! Repeat again. BLOW. Wait, wait. BLOW. Wait. BLOW again. Back in. Turn on! Yes, okay, the game is now up and loading on the TV! *But now I have to start all over again....*

Thus, finding the hidden ***Warp Whistles*** was crucial. In fact, it became a sort of obsessive fascination and game in-and-of-itself!

For example, one of the earlier *Warp Whistles* in the game was attained only by ingesting a green, magical "Super Leaf" and then, if adorned with a Raccoon Tail, you could fly high, high above the exit screen at the end of the level. Way out of sight, your Mario character couldn't even be seen. Yet you must continue flying! You must fly "off the screen" until absolute blackness was all you could see on the TV—only then, if you pressed the down button on the D-Pad, you'd suddenly be taken into a secret room containing a treasure box.

Inside the treasure box? You guessed it—a coveted *Warp Whistle*!

These *Whistles* were so valuable and so critical that their hidden locations would be the frenzied discussion at school each and every day. The other kids would regularly lie ("exaggerate") at the lunch table and tell you they stumbled across a heretofore never-before-known-about and BRAND-NEW *Warp Whistle* no one else had ever found; it would do *amazing* things you couldn't imagine. But, no, he couldn't possibly tell you its location or how to get to it! It was a secret he would take to his grave!

Nevertheless, these *Warp Whistles* and the secrets to discovering them were heavily coveted. They were discussed in hushed tones during class and yelled about boisterously at lunchtime. The mysteries of the *Warp Whistles* soon became even more exciting than playing the game itself!

Later in life, I found this fact very interesting to ponder. It was curious that this "game within the game" (seeking the hidden shortcuts) became more important than playing the real game. But that's more of a philosophical discussion, so I'll put that cerebral topic on the shelf for the time being....

Yet, here's the point. The *Warp Whistles* were such a central and critical part of gameplay that the thought of playing without using them was almost *heretical.* If some new kid joined the school and Mario 3 came up in conversation (and of course it would), then the first question asked was which *Warp Whistles* he preferred to use and why....

One day a new kid named Aaron Jenkins came to our school *(name changed to protect his honor and dignity)*. Our mutual love of Mario 3 came up in natural conversation. However, when he sheepishly admitted that he didn't even KNOW about these *Warp Whistles (!)*—it would have been better if he had come to school with three heads!! The mere notion of someone playing the game without knowing about the *Warp Whistles* was wild. It was a bizarre thought. It was profane.

"But how do you warp to World 9 after you get to World 4? For that matter ... how do you even get to World 4 without the World 1 Whistle???" Other kids were beginning to gather, their eyes wide with anticipation and shock.

"I ... guess I don't. I've never gotten that far. I like the water world mostly."

You could have heard a pin drop in that lunchroom.

The water level was World 3. *No one played the water level!* The *Warp Whistle* in World 1 skipped the water level entirely and ported you to World 4.

But ... but ... he didn't know that.

He didn't know he could skip to World 4. He didn't know he could skip to World 9. He didn't know ... *anything*!

Aaron was a *Mario* 3 luddite! He was a philistine.

Our young, inner consciences waged a war, battling the conflated concepts of incredulity, shock, and a desire for acceptance and new friendship all at once.

He just didn't know what he didn't know.

And who's fault was this, really? It's not like teachers taught us anything important in class all day, like where to discover new *Warp Whistles*. The sad truth slowly dawned on me:

It wasn't his fault he didn't know! And there's a lesson in that.

It's also a lesson for today's investors. Sometimes in life we just don't know what we don't know! The locations of life's financial *Warp Whistles* aren't public knowledge. What's worse, standard financial advisors and "conventional wisdom" train us to do exactly the opposite of what we did in Mario 3: *take amazing shortcuts that catapult us ahead of our peers and colleagues.*

Instead, "Conventional Wisdom" from financial experts advise us to play the investment game level by level, world by world. But here's the problem: they don't even know about the *Warp Whistles*; and perhaps wouldn't even tell us if they did.

So that's why I wrote this book! There are so many financial and investing *Warp Whistles* in life! They are invaluable. They are so easy to find and use once you know where to look!

Call it "cheating"—call it "beating the system"—or call it more aptly "playing the game to WIN according to the rules available."

But in one's financial plan, unlike in the NES game world, getting ahead and "winning" (gaining true **Financial Freedom**—see Chapter 6) can mean the difference between building generational wealth and working a 9-5 job from the day you graduate to the day you die.

So, I say this to you: don't play the game of investing without learning to find and then blow hard on those magical *Warp Whistles!* These tools are embedded in the fabric of the financial game itself. They are DESIGNED for you to use. You just need to know about them and how to use them.

I'll show you how ...

INTRODUCTION

So, before diving into the meat and potatoes, let's set a few ground rules and expectations.

First, *who is this book written for exactly?* Well, at the risk of sounding trite—it's for *everyone*. It's for YOU. After sharing a first draft of this book's manuscript, I had a dear friend genuinely ask me, *"But aren't I a bit too old to start all this now?"*

The answer, quite honestly, is **NO**! Regardless of your experience, age, past failures, or misconceptions about investing/speculating, it is *NEVER* too late to get on the right path. For as the ancient proverb says:

The BEST time to plant a tree was 30 years ago....
The next best time is ***now****!*

Yes, I believe I CAN teach an old dog new tricks. I believe I can properly reorient the *financially challenged* or *investor-illiterate*. It may be a bold claim, but I wouldn't have written this book if I didn't wholeheartedly believe I could make a difference and impart some wisdom in order to change lives!

Second, know this: in these chapters I'm going to unpack, to the best of my ability, the wisdom and philosophy of financial gurus FAR smarter than me from across many different financial tomes.

And in complete honesty, I'll probably do these authors a great disservice by distilling their robust messages into a few brief pages. These books DESERVE to be read and re-read. They deserve to be studied and analyzed. By reading this book *without* reading the authors and books I reference, you are getting a poorly written *'SparkNotes'* version of a Dickens classic. So please READ THE BOOKS I mention in the corresponding chapters.

That said, I understand in this fast-paced world it's hard to find the time to read 10 different books. Especially when you want to *GO, GO, GO*. I get it.

But I cannot stress enough how my words on these pages are merely regurgitated sludge; much smarter and far more eloquent writers have extolled the virtues of sound financial strategies in their own works. So then, once again: I HIGHLY, HIGHLY, HIGHLY recommend—no, **beg**—that you read the following books:

1. **The Richest Man in Babylon** by George S. Clason
2. **Rich Dad, Poor Dad** by Robert Kiyosaki
3. **The Cash Flow Quadrant** by Robert Kiyosaki
4. **Becoming Your Own Banker** by Nelson Nash
5. **The Case for IBC** by Carlos Lara and Robert Murphy
6. **How Privatized Banking Really Works** by Carlos Lara and Robert Murphy
7. **The Total Money Makeover** by Dave Ramsey
8. **Tax-Free Wealth (3rd Edition)** by Tom Wheelwright
9. **How an Economy Grows and Why It Crashes** by Peter Schiff
10. **Economics in One Lesson** by Henry Hazlitt
11. **The Lords of Easy Money** by Christopher Leonard
12. **The Dao of Capital** by Mark Spitznagel
13. **Principles for Dealing with the Changing World Order** by Ray Dalio
14. **What Would the Rockefellers Do?: How the Wealthy Get and Stay That Way, and How You Can Too** *by Garrett Gunderson*
15. **Choice: Cooperation, Enterprise, and Human Action** *by Robert P. Murphy*

Once you have read these amazing works, you will far better understand the concepts I describe in this book and be more convinced by their effectiveness than my simple ramblings will permit. That all said, if you don't have the time or interest and just want the "spark notes" version of these philosophies, fine. Just fine!

But fair warning: you'll be hearing through a muted amplifier a set of strategies that almost certainly will change your life forever and permit you to pay off debts faster, save more money than you thought possible, and invest far more wisely (and with less risk) than you ever imagined....

Lastly, my goal in writing this book is to simply "bring the horse to water," so to speak *(yes, you're the horse in that analogy)!* It's YOUR job to drink.

The advice is proven and verifiable. The *Warp Whistles* are real! Yes, many or most of the investment philosophies in these pages buck the trend and are novel or "different." But different is good! Normal is boring. We don't strive to be normal; we must strive to be ***exceptional***!

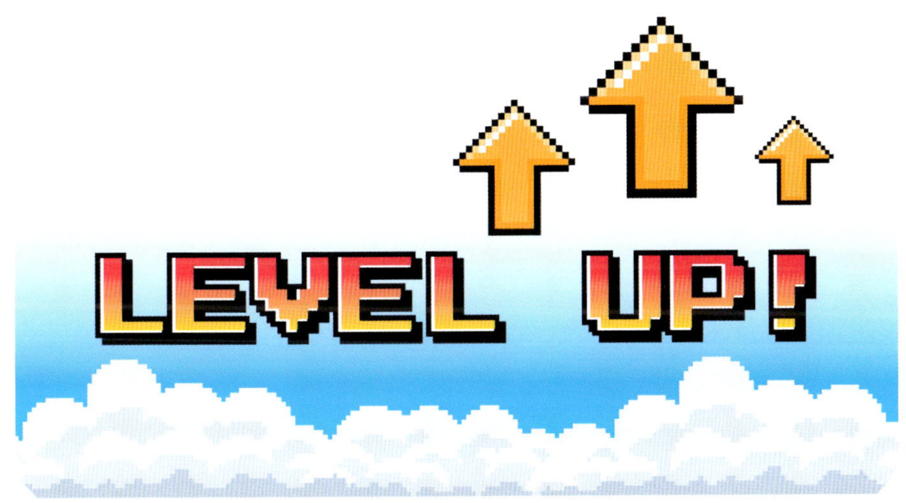

> *"An investment in knowledge pays the best interest."*
> —Benjamin Franklin

WARP
FOUND!
PLAYER 1

CHEAT CODE #1

A COMPLETE PARADIGM SHIFT (MINDSET REALIGNMENT)

I hate these stupid "mindset" chapters as much as the next guy. Probably more, in fact.

Frankly, I usually skip anything to do with **mindset** when reading books such as these. If I have to hear one more time how I need to *"change my thinking before I can change my life,"* I might just blow my brains out.

These so-called "self-help" chapters are dumb. So, I won't be giving you any nonsense or fluff. That's a solemn promise!

But I will say this: before one can build a house, he must build a foundation. And even before that, he must learn how to use his tools before he can apply them. *Yadda, yadda.* You get the point...

In plain English, if you begin reading the subsequent chapters of this book still believing the standard set of useless garbage that financial planners or "business school" taught you, you'll get absolutely nowhere. So, allow me just a quick chapter to help you *"unlearn what you have learned"* (yes, that's a *Master Yoda* quote and make no mistake about it!)

Shirk "Normal"!

Do you know what it means to be "normal"? By definition, it means *non-extraordinary.*

Regular....

Ordinary!

It means *doing what everyone else is doing.*

In statistics, it's "the mean" or the average. It's the vast majority under the 'bell curve'. It's all the people in the middle—those who don't stand out.

Because *the outliers* stand out; the 'Normal' people fit in and do what everyone else is doing.

In the world of finances, 'Normal' is believing or doing the following things:

- Go to college
- Work a stable 9-5 job
- Invest in your 401K ("plan for retirement")
- Save for your kid's college with a 529 Government Plan
- Pay down your mortgage early (or refinance to a 15Y)
- Defer gratification (to when you can afford it in retirement)
- Invest in the stock market with extra funds ("diversified portfolio" of course)
- Work until retirement age
- Hope and pray your qualified plan (401k/403b) is large enough when you retire so that you can **time it just right** to not use up all your money before you die!

(In fact, maybe you can die early so you can give your kids some sort of an inheritance. That would be nice ...) Read over the above items. Without exaggeration, this is the "Normal" list of general financial advice you'll get from any generic financial advisor. You'll also get this same advice from your friends, parents, and colleagues. Some of the advice might not be phrased as sarcastically as above, but the bones are the same.

This, supposedly, is just "smart financial advice." This is what 99% of America is doing. So why not do what's "normal?"

Well, the problem is—it's ***ALL*** wrong.

The entire paradigm of the 'normal' investor is 100% WRONG!

If you want to get ***extraordinary*** results, you don't accomplish that by doing what's "normal." You must be extraordinary. You must be unique. You have to take paths not routinely traveled; you must be **unusual**! Be *un-normal* or *anti-normal!*

To take advantage of a financial *Warp Whistle*, you don't play the levels in the game consecutively. You have to find the *cheat codes* that propel you faster and further along the track than what is considered acceptable and "normal."

"But isn't that risky?"

No. In fact, the OPPOSITE is true. It is quite counter-intuitive, but believe it or not, bucking the trend and investing properly is actually far **safer,** more **secure,** more **flexible,** and more **lucrative** than following the "conventional wisdom."

Beware Groupthink!

GROUPTHINK. (noun) *the practice of thinking or making decisions as a group, especially when this results in bad decisions being made.*

Oxford Learner's Dictionary

In the modern-day investing paradigm, *chasing yield* has become the "norm." It's NORMAL to seek returns in equity markets such as the stock market and through the government's qualified plans including the **401(k)**, the **403(b), Roth IRAs, SEP IRAs, etc.**

Mutual Funds diversify risk, but they still are just a collection of equities.

It is not possible to properly remove systemic risk by packaging a bunch of risky things together and then calling it magically safe! Mutual funds are just well-diversified packages of risk!

To see what I mean, consider this example from yesteryear. From 2000–2006 (and leading all the way up to the 2007/2008 financial collapse), it was "normal" for investors and even "conservative" pension funds to invest in tranches of A- and AA-rated subprime mortgages as well as (later) Collateralized Debt Obligations (CDOs)—which are just derivative instruments betting on the same underlying security.

Perhaps best explained in the movie The Big Short, banks were packaging up C- and D-rated subprime loans (aka "dog-shit," as explained in the film by Margot Robbie while soaking in a bathtub) into "diversified" bundles of dog-shit. The banks then went back to the rating agencies, who perfunctorily rated the entire bundle A, AA, and even AAA—since the bundles of dog-shit were now suddenly safe and "well diversified!"

This was all considered "normal investing" that the "conventional wisdom" fully endorsed and supported. The normal investor class didn't question things because groupthink was reinforcing their preconceived (yet false) assumptions that "going with the flow" was the right thing to do.

Again, this was what was "normal." This was what everyone was doing. Normal doesn't question the conventional wisdom. "Normal" does not question the majority! "Normal" does what everyone else is doing.

Yet, ironically, in this case going against the grain is 100% the right thing to do and provides LESS RISK, not more!

This is not to say that being counter-cultural or sailing against the tide is always the correct decision JUST because it is not what everyone else is doing. There is no intrinsic wisdom or brilliance in being an iconoclast for its own sake.

For example, betting on black when everyone else is betting on red is still just gambling. However, challenging the prevailing consensus is often wise, especially when you may believe groupthink has clouded people's ability for properly assessing risk. This is very common, as people tend to see their investment strategy with rose-colored glasses and often downplay the systemic risks involved, especially when the majority of others are in on the trade with them.

But remember: "there's safety in numbers" is a dirty lie and a *myth*!

Score-Carding Qualified Plans

Another reason to buck the common trends is when the investments being marketed offer little or no a) **control,** b) **flexibility,** or c) **collateral.** These three facets are critical in a sound investment strategy. Let's analyze the "Normal" 401(k)/403(b) investment strategy against these three litmus tests.

1. **Control.** It may be said that a 401(k) (or other qualified plans) gives some level of limited control in how the funds are invested (e.g., which mutual funds you select), but even when this is true, this is not what I mean when I refer to control. True control is how much **governance** you have over asset(s) both before AND after funds are invested. Do you have the ability to a) **control the asset purchase**, b) **sell the asset**, c) **modify/ manage the asset,** and d) **extricate funds** from the investment as needed? In this case, the scorecard is very poor against these metrics. Let's do a quick breakdown:

    a. **Control the Asset Purchase?—*PARTIALLY*** (limited). The investor often has a very limited range of mutual funds that can be selected for purchase. But if the investor wishes to purchase assets not available in the employer plan (e.g., real estate, etc.), he is out of luck! His control over his purchasing decisions is extremely limited.

    b. **Control to Sell the Asset?—*YES BUT NO.*** The investor has the ability to sell the equities as needed (although often there is a 24 72-hour window to execute trades, depending on the plan). HOWEVER, you *cannot* use that cash; you must simply let it sit "in cash" or use it to buy other risky assets.

    c. **Control to Modify/Manage the Asset?—*NO.*** With respect to equities and mutual funds, there is absolutely zero control over the assets being purchased. You are a stockholder (with limited voting rights, at best), but you have no ability to exert control or provide management direction for the companies for which you are a stockholder. Even when a shareholder desires to become informed or vote on critical company matters, there are a myriad obstacles. Proxy statements issued by corporations in advance of a shareholder meetings are *esoteric*, to say the least—and for most people are like reading Greek.

d. **Control to Extricate Funds?—*NO***. This is the most important element of control when the rubber meets the investment road. The investor in a 401(k) or other qualified plan has essentially *locked up his/her money for 30–40+ years*. Those monies are not accessible, and certainly cannot be extracted and used for other, more lucrative (and less risky) investment opportunities. Those dollars are essentially in "financial purgatory."

2. **Flexibility**. As mentioned above, the 401(k) and other qualified plans offer little by the way of flexibility. Kind of like Ford's original Model-T: "*you can get it in any color, as long as it's black*." The investor often gets the choice of 10–15 "flavors" of different mutual funds. If you're very lucky (and this is rare) you can opt to purchase individual equities within your plan. Or you may even be able to rollover your plan to a **Self-Directed IRA** in order to have a bit more flexibility and control (usually this is only after you voluntarily leave or are fired from your company).

   However, even then, when presented with a choice between different mutual funds (or even individual stocks), this is like choosing between a *turd sandwich* and a *turd salad*. Sure, that salad is healthier, but it still has turds in it!

   (By the way, for the remainder of this book I would suggest anytime you read the word "equities" you should translate it in your head to "turds.")

   <u>Nota Bene</u> ("NB", or "Take Note" in Latin): The inherent market risk involved with being over-allocated in equities (no matter how diversified they are) is ***quite high.***

   But getting back to **flexibility:** you have little to no control over the buy side when it comes to which asset class(es) you can purchase.

You'll likely get a so-called "broad spectrum" of choices such as **Small Cap Funds, Large Cap Funds, Value Funds, Growth Funds, Balanced Funds, International Funds, Bond Funds,** and then the ever-present options related to your age of retirement—which, in theory, should de-risk as you age (these are called **Target Date Funds).** That's your "flexibility."

Your range of options essentially is between *risky equities* (diversified) and *very, very risky equities* (diversified). However, the investor gets absolutely no ability to take advantage of highly lucrative investments such as real estate, private business ownership, managed funds, private loans, and many other amazing asset classes that offer **passive income, lower risk**, and much **higher returns** (not to mention tremendous **tax benefits)**. We'll get to all this and more in **Chapters 6 and 7**!

Nor are any promises made (in fact quite the opposite) about being able to take advantage of **uninterrupted compounding**.

Nor can the monies invested in the plan be removed; instead, they are kept locked away until the magic year in which you *graduate from work* and get to retire (assuming, that is, these risky investments are at a high-enough balance that allows you to retire—which assumes there haven't been significant "down years" to set your retirement plans back a decade or two).

3. **Collateral.** Last but not least, can you collateralize the assets in your 401(k)/403(b)?

   Collateralization of assets is one of the primary ways that the rich stay rich and get progressively richer. It is a *powerful* tool that every investor should learn about and take advantage of.

   Investors with leverage and the ability to collateralize can borrow against their assets in order to invest in low-risk, **cash flow-producing assets.** This powerful tool of **collateralization**, when available to an investor, can unlock a significant amount of potency from each and every dollar of their net worth.

   Collateralization is an extremely invaluable tool!

So then, can you collateralize the assets in your qualified plan...? The answer, of course—is **NO.** You cannot. The government does not allow this.

401(k) SCORECARD SUMMARY TIME!

So then ... let's summarize. The funds "invested" in a qualified plan face the following limitations:

1. **Control:** Funds locked up for 30-40 years ("financial purgatory");
2. **Flexibility:** Restrained to a very narrow and limited number of asset classes (i.e., only equities and mutual funds);
3. **Collateralizable: NOT** collateralizable;
4. **Risk:** Risky (or **extremely** risky, depending on your elections);

In short, qualified plans fail the "sniff test" by every conceivable metric. Yet, despite all this, everyone and their grandmother will tell you they're the best thing since sliced bread. *"You'd be a fool not to contribute to your 401(k) ..."*

What *Normal* People Think and Do

But millions of people can't be wrong, can they? *There's safety in numbers, right?*

With these questions ringing in the mind of all new employees, the 401(k)/403(b) plans are so pervasive in society that it is rare to see any "normal" person dare try anything else. Why buck the trend? Well, part of the reason for this is simply a lack of education and a lack of exposure to other viable options.

Adding salt to the wound, famed economic wizards such as **Nobel Prize** winner Richard Thaler have implemented so-called "Nudge Theory" in the space of qualified plan election during the onboarding process of new employment. Instead of having the election process default to NO—meaning the new employee must OPT IN to a 401(k) plan with his/her company—the new paradigm, as of 2006, is that employees are **automatically enrolled** in their company's program and thus needs to take extra steps to OPT OUT in order to consciously not participate in the plan.

This seemingly small, but important, "nudge" is key because it accents the gentle yet insidious goal by governments to push people *en masse* to participate in *groupthink* and "just go with the flow!" It is a prime example of government and Wall Street colluding for financial gain in order to do what they prescribe is "right" for the employee. However, they provide only a false sense of financial and investment security while at the same time *bolstering the stock market* (a proxy for economic growth).

Pompeii's Example

The citizens of Pompeii, living in the shadow of an active volcano, were confident in their future. They rarely concerned themselves with the shakes and tremors of the angry mountain. They became accustomed to the shaking land, just as investors today balk at "minor market tremors" (labeling them "normal volatility.")

So too, wise and "learned'" men on CNBC calmly pacify the normal investor, explaining that the market goes down and then comes back up; but it all "*averages out!*" The strength of the market is "*sound,*" and the "normies" should not be swayed by the "normal ups and downs" of the marketplace. It's all just normal. So very *normal.*

Normal, Normal, Normal...

In the end, "normal" means a lot of unanticipated things for the typical investor they don't think about. It means *complacency*. It means *apathy*. It means *"set it and forget it"* and *no engagement* with respect to their investments.

What it means is ***mediocrity*****!**

When all you do is squirrel your money away in a 401(k) plan, you don't need to *actively participate* in your financial future. Because, as mentioned above, **YOU HAVE NO CONTROL.**

But why worry about things you can't control, right? The market goes up and down. It goes down and back up again.

Financial "gurus" like Jim Cramer say *"just ride the waves. It'll average out!"*

"Conventional Wisdom" promises that by the time you retire, you'll have a fat nest-egg and can be comfortable. Until then, keep your head down, don't worry about things, and work hard. Your hard work and "doing what everyone else is doing" will pay off!

The problem with this mentality is that without **flexibility, control,** and **collateral,** your "normal" investment strategy will always be subpar AND be subject to massive **systemic risk.** And you won't even know it!

Sure, your financial advisor will send you cute little letters once a month detailing how well your investments are doing (or in the down months he'll downplay the problems as "temporary setbacks").

But I'm here to tell you that "normal" is frightening. "Normal" is *risky*. "Normal" is all about having a **Scarcity Mindset** instead of having an **Abundance Mindset.**

Most pernicious of all, "normal" standardizes *complacency* and removes any onus of taking control of your financial future! That is very dangerous. No one should care more about your financial future than **YOU**; if you delegate this responsibility to some financial advisor (or, worse, just some mindless group of mutual funds) then *you have abdicated your God-given role as master of your own financial destiny.* That is truly depressing.

So that's "Normal." What, then, can we do to make ourselves "Un-Normal…"?

Be Un-Normal. Be Extraordinary!

I just spent a lot of time describing "normal." And it was surprisingly easy because it's what nearly everybody is currently doing. Normal is someone working hard in a W2 job, keeping their head down, and not worrying a lick about **buying assets** or **creating passive income**….

Worse yet, they're "over-risked" as well as *overly confident* in their strategy because they have *groupthink*, the safety of numbers, and the backing of all the "smartest people in the room" giving them *attaboys*.

I'm sad to admit it, but here's the truth: the "normal" people are all doing everything completely *backwards*! So, let's explore how to be un-normal. Let's be weird. Strange. Provocative, even. ***Extraordinary***!

Let's see how we can take the path less travelled and build a system that **creates generational wealth, reduces risk, escapes taxes**, and allows complete **financial freedom** without gambling in the "Wallstreet Casino."

We shall explore all of these concepts and more in the following chapters....

Audentes Fortuna iuvat!
"Fortune favors the bold!"
–Virgil

NASDAQ
401K
RISK LVL
4
AIR BNB
RISK LVL
3
RISK LVL
2
FOR RENT
RISK LVL
1
PLAYER 1

CHEAT CODE #2

THE WEALTH PYRAMID

Investing vs. Speculating

Let's take a quick second to define some basic terms.

Investing (aka "Income Investing") is when you put money into an asset that will consistently pay a return based on some known frequency. This could be one of three (3) primary varieties:

1. The asset pays regular and *consistent* **dividends** (such as a corporation's STABLE dividend, a company's *Guaranteed Payment*, or *certain* managed fund distributions)
2. The asset pays regular **coupon** or **loan** payments (such as a bond or income from private lending)
3. The asset pays regular **rental income** (i.e., leasing real estate)

If it does not check one of the three boxes above, it is NOT an investment. Instead, it very likely is **speculative** in nature. This is not in any way "bad," *per se*. However, it is very important to properly define terms to ensure we do not conflate **investing** with **speculating**.

Speculation is when you put money into financial assets, such as non-dividend-paying stocks, real estate, commodities, or currencies, with the primary goal of achieving significant short-term profits based on **anticipated price movements.**

Unlike traditional investing, which focuses on long-term growth and income generation based on an asset's intrinsic value, speculation involves taking on higher risk, often relying on **market trends, rumors,** or **predictions about future price changes**. Speculators often buy assets they believe will increase in value or sell assets they expect to decrease, aiming to capitalize on these fluctuations.

This will all become more important below, where I define and break down the Tiers within the Pyramid of Wealth and how to allocate capital according to specific target allocation percentages.

The Pyramid of Wealth

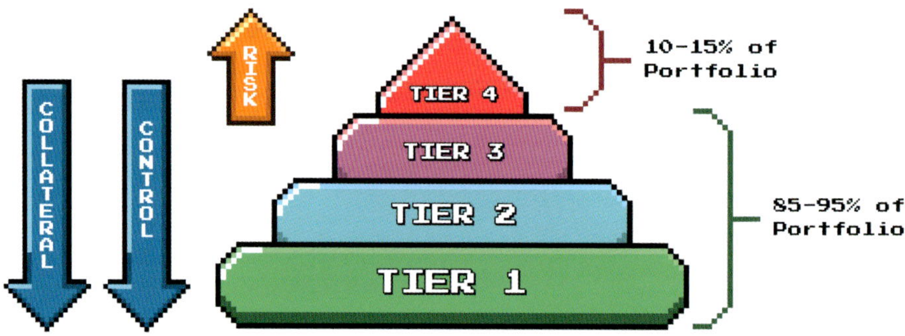

In my not-so-humble opinion, the most central part of one's investing mantra is knowledge of, and adherence to, **The Wealth Pyramid.**

The premise is super simple, but also quite controversial—given that it is nearly the opposite of what all the "normal" people are doing.

The **Wealth Pyramid** has four Tiers (or tranches), which represent different types of Asset Classes. As one moves "up" from the bottom level, one's control decreases, as does the ability to **collateralize** the asset.

The very bottom tier, **Tier 1**, should represent the BULK of one's financial wealth. It's the thickest part of the pyramid for a reason. It contains the safest (least risky) assets, and they are typically the most liquid as well.

The investor maintains **complete control** and can **fully collateralize** these assets if needed. Your cash-value whole life insurance and other easily sellable assets like gold, silver, or bonds are in this tranche. More on **Whole Life Insurance** in Chapter 5: Build Your Infinite Banking System!

Moving upward, **Tier 2** represents assets where control and collateral are reduced. For example, long-term rental properties may be in this tier. These assets are still collateralizable but may be more difficult to sell or manage. This tier may also contain well-established, cash flow-producing seasoned businesses. One should be expected to hold as much as ***50–80%*** of their net wealth just in Tiers 1 and 2.

Tier 3 contains assets like short-term rental properties, managed funds, personal loans, or businesses that are not seasoned (e.g., startups). It also contains dividend-paying stocks (or even certain "value stocks" when appropriate). One might be expected to hold ***10–20%*** of their net wealth in this tranche.

Tier 4 is SPECULATION and no longer represents investing. In this tier are assets in which you can exert no control whatsoever and have no ability to impact long-term results. They are "hit or miss" *gambles*. These might include speculation in cryptocurrencies, stocks, and mutual funds (even if diversified). **NB:** a prudent investor should hold no more than ***10–15%*** of their net worth in this tier!

When looking at the asset allocations prescribed by the **Wealth Pyramid,** the typical ("Normal") person's pyramid is completely *flipped upside down* from what's shown. Most American investors, as mentioned, hold 80%+ of their net worth within a risky 401(k). That's equities. That's ***speculation***—not investing!

As depicted, speculative assets are at the **TOP** of the pyramid for a reason—they're in Tier 4!

These assets provide zero collateral and no flexibility/control.

They should make up the *minority* of one's wealth, not the bulk of it.

For if you flipped the **Wealth Pyramid** upside down (as many people unfortunately do), it loses all stability and is poorly structured for handling risk.

A breakdown of the various asset classes and in which tranche of the Wealth Pyramid they reside is listed as follows:

Tier	Asset Class(es)	Risk	Control	Collateralizable	% Allocation
Tier 1	Cash Value Life Insurance, Commodities, Savings	NONE	YES	YES	25-50%
Tier 2	Multi-Family Real Estate, Established/Seasoned Businesses	LOW	YES	YES	25-50%
Tier 3	Managed Funds, Private Loans, Short-Term Rentals ("STRs"), Certain Equities (Dividend-Paying)	MED	NO	SOME	10-20%
Tier 4	Equities (401Ks), Crypto, Businesses (Speculative or Startups), Gambling	HIGH	NO	NO	0-15%

As should be obvious, the higher you go up the pyramid, the fewer dollars should be invested in each respective Tier.

These are the rules of the pyramid:

1. **Control** decreases as you move up.
2. **Collateralization ability** decreases as you move up.
3. **Risk** increases as you move up.

However, what's notable is although risk increases as you ascend the Pyramid, this does NOT necessarily correlate to an increase in the **rate of investment return!**

Once again, bucking conventional wisdom, *it is a MYTH that you need to take more risk in order to achieve higher returns.* My personal experience, as well as that of the authors detailed in this book, demonstrates quite the opposite in fact. An investor can often make *far better returns* residing near the BOTTOM of the pyramid than at the top!

As one stays near the BOTTOM of the pyramid (specifically in Tier 2, where multi-family real estate and seasoned businesses resides), this is the "sweet spot" tier for asset classes that experience the **highest returns** and the **lowest risks.**

In short, one does not need to "chase yield" by taking greater and greater risks. Quite the opposite!

Many of my personal investments in businesses as well as real estate provide stable, consistent, and highly profitable returns (with assets that are fully collateralized). You can't say the same of Tier 4 assets!

Alternatively, I would have had to put 6–10x the amount of capital in equity markets (Tier 4) to achieve the same return as putting capital in Tier 2 assets; and, if I did so, I would also be taking on 10–20x the amount of risk!

Call me crazy, but I would prefer to see **GREATER RETURNS** while taking **LESS RISK.** This is why I choose to live in this "sweet spot" of Tier 2 assets for the vast majority of my assets and investments. The target percentage allocations recommended by the **Wealth Pyramid** do not disappoint!

Lastly, a small word of nomenclature with respect to the Tiers:

- ☆ Tier 1—**WEALTH PRESERVATION** (not investing)
- ☆ Tier 2—**INVESTING**
- ☆ Tier 3—**RISKIER INVESTING**
- ☆ Tier 4—**SPECULATION** (not investing)

It should be noted that only two of the four tiers (the middle two) actually deal with investing at all!

The assets in Tier 1 primarily focus on **Flexibility, Liquidity,** and **Wealth Preservation.** Capital in Tier 1 is used to FUND lucrative investments in Tiers 2, 3, and 4 (see Chapter 6: Create Passive Income Streams).

Tier 1 is also the one and only tier where ***certainty*** exists. The "wealth preservation" assets in Tier 1 should provide stability and certainty of returns at a "risk-free" or near risk-free rate. This is why Cash Value (CV) life insurance, gold/silver, and other stable/reliable assets belong here.

Pesky Pareto! Beware the 80/20 Rule

Take heed of the 80/20 rule—also called the *Pareto Principle.*

Generically, the principle states that 80% of effects are often due to 20% of the causes. This can be a good thing or a bad thing—or a neutral thing.

For example:

- ☆ 80% of a company's sales may come from 20% of its products.
- ☆ 20% of customers may lead to 80% of the total complaints.
- ☆ 80% of a company's income may come from 20% of its customers.

These Pareto distributions are quite common in life as well as in business—and also in investing. But with respect to the **Wealth Pyramid,** *you must take care to avoid the Pareto Principle* when allocating capital in the respective Tiers!

For nothing better embodies the "normal" investor than the **Pareto Principle!**

Eighty percent or more of a *normal* person's capital is typically locked up in 20% of the **Wealth Pyramid** (specifically in Tier 4 Speculative assets (i.e., "the top of the Pyramid")!

The danger of focusing 80% of one's time, energy, focus, and/or capital on the TOP of the Pyramid (in Speculative assets) has hopefully been made abundantly clear so far. However, I will continue to drive this point home throughout the book.

In fact, when one examines the stock market through the lens of **"Investing vs. Speculating,"** fewer than 15% of all stocks in the S&P 500 would classify as "Investments" under the definition explained earlier in this chapter. Looking at data, only 66 stocks in the S&P 500 (13.2%) classify as "Dividend Aristocrats"—stable companies that have paid (and increased) their dividends for at least 25 consecutive years (S&P Global).

Estimates of the total number of publicly traded stocks in the U.S. vary depending on the sources and criteria used (e.g., including or excluding OTC markets). However, as a rough estimate, there are around 4,000 to 6,000 publicly traded stocks across all U.S. exchanges. Let's take a midpoint estimate of 5,000 U.S. stocks for calculation purposes:

$$\text{Percentage} = \left(\frac{\text{66 Dividend Aristocrats}}{\text{5000 Total U.S. Stocks}}\right) \times 100 \approx 1.32\%$$

Thus, from this perspective, only around 1.32% of total U.S. stocks are *investments*. The rest are primarily *speculative* in nature.

Given this vantage point, I strongly encourage you not to become distracted by the noise around the water cooler. Don't buy into the hype when it comes to making exciting stock picks, nor be obsessed with *chasing yield* in lucrative opportunities.

This buzzing is obsessed with the cherry on top (the top of the Pyramid) but completely ignores the cake (the bottom of the Pyramid)! People who obsess about equity markets and growth stock investing are missing the forest for the trees!

In Homer's *The Odyssey*, Odysseus and his crew sail past the island Anthemoessa on their long travel back home. By its shoals live *the sirens*! These were mythical creatures—part bird, part woman—whose enchanting music and voices lured sailors to their doom. Drawn by the irresistible allure of their song, sailors would steer their ships toward the Sirens, only to crash on the rocky coastlines and perish.

Allocating 80% or more of one's capital in Tier 4 of the Wealth Pyramid is a Siren's song to most investors! Speculating has become "normal." This is what everyone else is doing. And to be clear—there is nothing inherently wrong with speculating. Risk is a fun and exciting part of life and investing. *But overbalancing the* **top** *of your Pyramid with equities comes with a high risk of steering your ship against the rocks.*

Those sirens and their numinous songs are alluring! The water cooler is abuzz with doe-eyed sailors, lost on rough investing seas, enchanted by their voices.

Bitcoin ETFs!

AI companies!

Penny stocks!

Cryptocurrencies!

Growth stock mutual funds in a 401(k)!

Siren songs, all.

Speculating can be exciting. It can even make you a TON of money if you're lucky and time your investments just right. But you're just as likely to crash your vessel against the rocks and be eaten as you are to survive and live to tell the tale.

So, to reiterate, speculative assets like non-dividend-paying stocks, crypto, and mutual funds should represent no more than 15% (*max*) of your portfolio! Even a diversified stock portfolio is extremely risky. It is *speculating*, not investing.

Speculate if you wish; *nothing is wrong with it at all!* I speculate a small portion of my wealth (less than 15%) in Tier 4 assets—as shown in the "Application" section of this book. But just *call a spade a spade.*

More importantly, be sure to properly allocate both your time/energy as well as your capital according to the distribution of asset classes wisely described by the **Wealth Pyramid!**

I encourage you to disregard the Pareto Principle and spend *80–95%+ of your attention and capital laser-focused on Tiers 1–3*—the *lower* sections of the **Wealth Pyramid.**

The Wealth Pyramid is shaped the way it is for a reason; the bottom is the most stable part and makes up the BASE and MAJORITY of the shape. This is where you'll make the *highest returns for the lowest risk.*

Lastly, be sure to build up your liquid Tier 1 assets so you always have a pool of capital (your "bank") from which to invest. More on that in Chapter 5: Build Your Infinite Banking System....

Let's Summarize

Ok, so we covered a lot. Let's put it all together.

First, sound investing involves four critical points and pursuits:

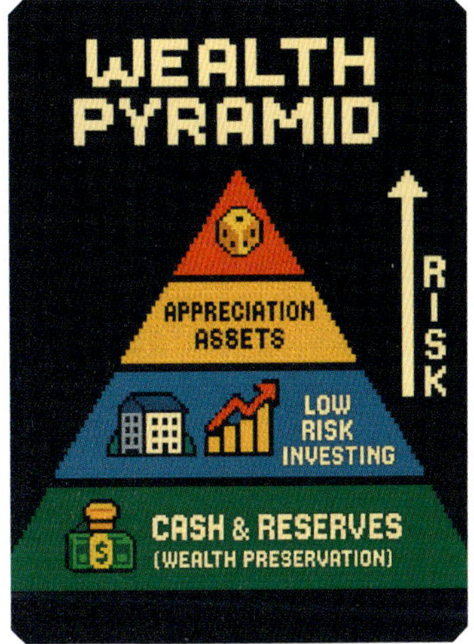

1. Understand the **Wealth Pyramid** and its four tiers (with the vast majority of assets being in the *lowest* 3 Tiers).

2. **Hoard/Save Tier 1 capital** as the base of your pyramid to use for investing in Tiers 2, 3, and 4
   - Note: in Chapter 5 you'll learn how to do this through a powerful banking vehicle ("IBC") that allows you to take advantage of uninterrupted, tax-free compounding (without the risk of loss).

3. Avoid the siren's song of gambling / speculating (Tier 4 of the Wealth Pyramid) with **more than 5-15%** of your net worth (i.e., this is putting money into the stock market, mutual funds, 401(k), crypto, etc.)

Understanding the **Wealth Pyramid** and using it to influence your asset allocation is very rewarding. It's one of the most powerful *Warp Whistles* in your arsenal; once blown, it will warp you miles ahead of those who exclusively gamble their money in risky equities (aka the stock market).

It's so much more exciting (and less risky!) to invest in **cash flow-producing assets** than trying to time the market or 'luck out' by chasing yield with speculative pursuits. More on this in Chapter 6....

"Speculation is most dangerous when it looks easiest."
—Warren Buffet

+1UP
LEVEL UP!
PLAYER 1

CHEAT CODE #3

GET OUT OF DEBT AND AVOID OVER-SPECULATING

Before one can invest and grow their wealth, they need to be out of personal debt (e.g., large balances on credit cards, medical debt, etc.). So, let's quickly cover the basics on that front before diving into the fun stuff. If you're 100% out of debt already, I give you full permission to skip ahead.

How to Get Out of (Bad) Debt!

Dave Ramsey—who doles out solid financial advice "your grandmother would give you"—posits a plan for getting out of debt fast and reaching a state of living that allows for maximum wealth growth.

At a high level he puts a plan in place whereby you "live like no one else so you may start living like no one else." Specifically, his philosophy is a super simplistic one and underscores the value of deferred gratification; if you budget correctly, you won't spend outside your means. If you spend within your means and cut back on all but the most essential, you'll be able to get out of debt and accumulate wealth faster than you ever thought possible.

That said, the most powerful components of his 7-step plan ("baby steps") are the initial 3½ steps. After that it's my staunch (and always accurate) opinion that his plan falls off the rails, and I shall explain why below.

But that's not to say throw the baby (steps) out with the bathwater! The power of the first 3½ steps is so incredible that if you follow those and ignore everything else, you'll set yourself up for success on a level that blows 99% of your peers, family, and neighbors out of the water.

Once you get past baby step #3 of Ramsey's plan, that is when you can find and unlock a crucial **Warp Whistle: Paying Yourself First** (keep reading below).

A quick word of warning: while it's true that Ramsey advocates strongly for investments in equities ("high-growth mutual funds"), I find this analogous to gambling one's money at a craps table (see Chapters 1 and 2). Instead, when reading his book, I firmly advocate to IGNORE everything Dave says about investing and only focus on his advice when it comes to debt relief (baby steps 1–3).

The **Warp Whistle** Dave sadly misses is that long-term wealth comes NOT from the stock market (speculation), but from saving and prudent investing in **passive income streams** (more on this in chapters to come). So please keep reading....

The Ramsey Plan in a Nutshell

The power of the Ramsey plan isn't in its sophistication or its uniqueness; it's in the sheer audacity of its simplicity. Like a classic Beatles song or Pink Floyd album, the best was best for a reason. And you just can't improve upon a classic.

Dave has several core philosophies of his plan which I'll quickly itemize:

1. **Budget! Budget! Budget!** Proper monthly budgeting allows you to see where your money goes; and, more importantly, it will give every dollar a name each month. If you don't accurately and honestly budget, you'll never get out of debt; it's that simple. If you're serious about getting out of debt, create and stick to a budget!
2. **Sacrifice Is Key to Reward.** "Live like no one else so you can later live and give like no one else." You don't need to keep up with the Joneses. Let them be—they're broke. If you sacrifice now, you'll be in a FAR better place later.
3. **Godly Financial Principles.** The Bible talks more about money than almost any other topic. Money is not the root of all evil; "love of money" is. Money is a tool. But like all tools (e.g., a gun or a hammer) it can be—and often is—very badly misused.

4. **Giving Money Is More Fun than Hoarding Money.** Amassing wealth does not mean you hoard it all for yourself. It allows you to give it away to those in need, tithe, and offer it to God/others in a way that has powerful effects. Because the weak can't support the weak, you can't help someone else until you're on solid footing yourself.

5. **Financial Freedom / Financial Peace.** Until you are financially free, and money isn't controlling your life, you are in bondage. Getting out of debt and equipping yourself for fiscal success will lead to peace. Nothing causes more fights or destroys relationships like money (and the lack thereof).

6. **Cash Is King. Credit Cards Are for Poor People.** When you're in debt, you cannot "beat" the system. There is no product in Earth's history that has been more aggressively marketed than the credit card. Credit card companies employ every gimmick, trick, and ploy in the book to get and keep you in debt; when you use charge-cards to pay for stuff, you pay more than you would otherwise.

The basic tenants of Dave's plan are broken down in very elemental "steps"—he calls them "baby steps"—which are a throwback from the movie *What about Bob* (another classic). Basically, you can't get from one place to another without taking small, incremental steps.

1. **Step 1** of the Ramsey plan is to *stop everything else* and build up as fast as possible $1,000 in an intermediary "Emergency Fund."

   This allows for the miscellaneous "gotchas" that come up all the time in our lives—like a car repair or a stove on the fritz. He understands and advocates the truth that you can't focus on saving or getting out of debt when you're being drowned by life. Getting this safety net in place allows you "breathing room" if/when something comes up.

2. **Step 2** involves getting out of debt via the "Debt Snowball." This is, in my opinion, the *most important part of the Ramsey plan.* Until you're out of debt, you are essentially a slave and don't have the monetary horsepower to quickly propel you to any real level of financial freedom.

   Dave suggests listing your debts in progressive order, from smallest to largest **(NOT including your mortgage).** Ignore interest rates for now.

Start paying your debts off in that order—starting with the lowest debt first—paying the minimum payments on all other debts. You want to focus on the emotional and psychological wins over a minutia of a few percentage points.

Once you have your first/lowest debt out of the way, use the momentum (same payment amount) and add it to pay for the next debt in line. As you work the Debt Snowball, you'll find it gets easier and easier as you move from one debt to the next.

Make sure that any credit cards you're paying off you're then cutting up. In fact, don't even wait to pay off the card—cut up the card NOW! The only good credit card is a cut-up and cancelled credit card. I don't care if you get 3,000 airline points for each purchase; you won't get rich amassing credit card miles. Getting out of debt while maintaining one or more credit cards is like trying to run a marathon while wearing metal boots. Why struggle with extra weight you don't need?

3. **Step 3.** By the time you get to baby step #3 you'll have accomplished one of the most critical financial steps/goals in your life: you're now out of debt. This is no small feat. It took herculean effort! By most accounts, people spend their *entire life* in debt. To be debt-free makes you "weird" and goes against the grain of normal society. But now it's time to bolster up that Emergency Fund....

   The initial Emergency Fund (from Step #1) was for the small stuff. Hopefully in your time working through Step #2, you didn't have to dip into it too much. But you might have to—and that puts you back to Step 1 until you've weathered the storm. Going through that may make you realize that some storms are bigger than others.

   To account for this, getting your Emergency Fund up to 6–12 months' worth of living expenses is what's next on the plan. The math for this is super easy, and completely depends upon your specific situation.

   If you have $4,000/mo in living expenses (food, gas, rent, etc.) then you'll want an emergency fund of $24,000–$48,000.

   Whether or not you opt for 6 months or 12 months of expenses is a tad arbitrary (and depends on your tolerance for risk/safety); also, if you have irregular income (e.g., rely on commissions, overtime, etc.) you might want to err on the side of more additional safety / more savings.

Make sure to store this Emergency Fund in something LIQUID (see Chapter 5: Build Your Infinite Banking System). Everything over and above this amount you can then use for the fun part: **INVESTING!**

So that's how you get out of debt and stay out of debt! Pretty neat, eh?

It should be noted here that the "Dave Ramsey Plan" for getting out of debt is FANTASTIC. It's probably the single most important thing anyone should do. So, if you're in debt, please *go back to read and re-read the previous section.* And follow through with the steps described!

However, everything after this in Ramsey's book (should you decide to read it)—*IGNORE!* I say this with humility, but Dave is flat out WRONG when it comes to all the subsequent "Baby Steps" after the first 3–4 steps.

For example, Dave advocates Step 4 as putting "15% of your household income into investments." So, while I agree capital should flow into investments (see all remaining chapters!), I don't think 15% is the right percentage (should be much higher!) and I also adamantly disagree with Dave's specific "investment" (read: speculation) approach.

Dave sadly advocates a "Normal" investment strategy—i.e., growth stock mutual funds and other speculative products!

Unfortunately, these asset classes all fall squarely into the category "equities" which are inherently *extremely risky* (aka "dog shit," see Chapter 1).

I don't believe anyone should GAMBLE their retirement income in the stock market—where people can (and do) lose 20% ... 25% ... 40%+ of their net worth overnight!

I believe a far ***safer*** *strategy is prudent when one's retirement is at stake.* The closer to retirement age you are, the less you can afford to have your wealth tied up in Tier 4 (speculative) assets (see Chapter 2: The Wealth Pyramid).

Building **passive income** is a far better approach to pursue. Don't worry; I will explain a lot more about this in Chapter 6!

It's DUMB to Pay Off/Down Your Mortgage—DON'T DO IT!

Okay, so please allow me to get on a brief soapbox about what is probably one of my biggest financial pet-peeves: people who choose to PAY OFF/DOWN THEIR MORTGAGES EARLY.

Ugh!! *Ahhhhhhhhhh*! This makes me so upset to see!

Whenever I hear people are doing this (or even thinking of doing this) I literally shutter and then vomit in my mouth a little bit!

I can't help but think of all the poor, innocent dollars being essentially tortured and abused—mercilessly consumed by the Big Banks (who smile with wicked grins at the stupidity of their customers).

Do Not Pay Off Your Mortgage Early!

Do not contribute an extra DIME to your mortgage to help "pay it down" before you retire! Do not refinance from a 30Y into a 15Y! *Only a financial DUNCE pays down their low-interest mortgage!!*

On their face, these seemingly innocuous financial practices seem sensible and responsible; however, in reality, these are some of the absolute *stupidest things you can do* with your poor, defenseless and undeserving-of-being-molested dollars! Please don't be so cruel!

Now, some of you may be thinking to yourself "But isn't this a Dave Ramsey chapter?" It did start off that way, didn't it?

Well, it's not one anymore, baby! Like I said earlier, when considering his "Baby steps," there is a hard stop at baby step #3! Everything after that is bunk! The power of Ramsey's plan is ONLY in the first 3 steps. You can ignore the rest and ignore pretty much everything else he says!

For example, I know Dave Ramsey posits that a "paid off home mortgage" is the sign of prosperity and financial freedom. Well, I'm here to tell you quite flatly—he's **100% WRONG**. He's so very wrong. Empirically. Mathematically. Logically. In every possible way—he's *wrong*.

Let's break this down a bit to clarify my position. For starters, most homeowners these days have a **LOW INTEREST MORTGAGE.** It's not just low. It's EPICLY low. It's subfloor in your basement low. Looking up the stats reveals the following interesting factoids:

- As of September 2024, approximately **62%** of American homeowners with mortgages have **a rate below 4%!** This figure represents a significant portion of the population who locked in lower rates before the sharp increases that began in 2022.
- As of September 2024, approximately **23%** of American homeowners with mortgages have **a rate below 3%!!** This group benefited from historically low rates primarily during the peak refinancing periods in 2020 and 2021, when the average mortgage rate dipped to around 2.96%.
- As of September 2024, the average mortgage rate for a 30-year fixed-rate loan is now around **6.35%** (S&P Global).

I wish I did not need to point out the obvious here, but mortgage rates less than 4% (62% of homeowners) or less than 3% (23% of homeowners) are INSANELY LOW. These rates represent an historical anomaly which likely will never occur again (at least not in our lifetimes or the lifetimes of our children or their children).

Banks are now literally KICKING themselves for making these fixed, low-interest, long-term commitments. They would do almost anything to get out of these bad loans (good for homeowners, but bad for banks because they lock up capital—which is now far, far more expensive).

So, the LAST thing you want to do is to let the big banks WIN and have exactly what they want: for you to pay down (or off) a low-interest mortgage!

Put another way, your ***mortgage*** *(not your house) is likely one of your most valuable assets!*

Let's analyze this further. Why is someone's low-interest mortgage more valuable than their house?? I will enumerate at least five reasons:

1. Financial Leverage

- ☆ A mortgage with a low-interest rate allows homeowners to borrow money cheaply.
- ☆ For instance, if a homeowner has a mortgage with an interest rate of 2.5%, they are effectively borrowing money at a cost significantly below the historical average. This low cost of borrowing allows homeowners to *allocate their money to other investments* that most assuredly will offer **higher returns.**
- ☆ For example, if a real estate investment yields a return of even 3% or more, the homeowner is making a net gain by **investing** rather than paying off or down his mortgage. (FYI the average ROI on a multi-family rental property is actually between **6–12% annually**).

2. Inflation Protection:

- ☆ A fixed-rate mortgage at a low interest rate is a *hedge against inflation.*
- ☆ Over time, inflation erodes the real value of debt, meaning the money paid back in the future is worth less than it is today.
- ☆ If a homeowner has a mortgage at 2.5% and inflation is running at 3% or higher (and today it is FAR higher than 3%!), *the real cost of that debt decreases over time.*
- ☆ This scenario allows homeowners to pay off their mortgage with "cheaper" dollars in the future!

3. Opportunity Cost:

- ☆ The opportunity cost of using capital to pay off a mortgage instead of investing it in higher-yielding opportunities is a significant consideration.
- ☆ As mentioned in #1, if the homeowner uses extra funds to pay down a 2.5% mortgage instead of **investing** in an asset that could return 12.5%+ annually, they are missing out on a 10.0% return!

4. Liquidity and Flexibility:

- ☆ Having a low-interest mortgage provides liquidity and financial flexibility.
- ☆ Homeowners can maintain a **cash reserve** (i.e., within an IBC Policy, see Chapter 5) or invest in other opportunities without being forced to lock up capital in their home's equity.
- ☆ This liquidity can be especially valuable in times of financial uncertainty or to seize investment opportunities.

5. Tax Benefits of Mortgage Interest Write-off:

- ☆ Although the tax benefits of mortgage interest have been reduced in recent years for certain homeowners, the interest on a mortgage is often **tax-deductible**—reducing the taxpayers' end-of-year tax bill.
- ☆ This write-off further bolsters the opportunity cost as well as the ROI of alternative investment approaches (since, on top of not investing and gaining the additional return, you would ALSO lose the tax benefit of the mortgage interest write off by paying off or paying down the mortgage early).

Choosing to pay down one's low-interest mortgage demonstrates:

1. A scarcity mindset,
2. A lack of financial understanding,
3. An utter lack of creativity, and
4. A (perceived) lack of alternative options for the capital.

To use an analogy, paying down a low interest mortgage is like going to an all-you-can-eat buffet filled with hundreds of new foods you could try—but you choose instead to eat a bowl of Cheerios.

Perhaps it's a poor example, but it shows a complete disregard for the possibilities available!

I put this section in the "Get Out of Debt" chapter because I wanted to leave no room for confusion about this topic.

Your mortgage debt is **NOT** *"bad debt!"*

Your low-interest mortgage is very *good debt.*

In fact, a low interest 30Y fixed mortgage is "GREAT debt." It's enviable debt. It's *valuable* debt which will propel you further ahead, especially as you pursue **passive income streams** (more to come on that in Chapter 6: Create Passive Income Streams).

To conclude this rant, I'll admit some misinformed people like Dave Ramsey will falsely tell you that paying off your home mortgage is a prudent financial decision.

It is not!

Paying off/down their mortgage is one of the all-time WORST things an investor can do with their hard-earned capital.

Remember instead:

- ☆ The value of a low-interest mortgage lies in its ability to provide cheap leverage, protect against inflation, and offer **financial flexibility.**
- ☆ This makes your mortgage potentially more valuable than your home itself in certain economic conditions!

Do not—I repeat: DO NOT—pay off your mortgage early, refinance your mortgage, or direct a single red penny more to your principal each month than you contractually must.

Every dime you spend "paying down" your mortgage is a dime that CAN'T be used for far bigger and better investment opportunities, such as growing your wealth through **passive income streams** (again, more on that in Chapter 6)....

Weathering Economic Storms

Due to the current political and financial climate, the American stock market is poised for a reckoning (perhaps the entire banking sector at large). Our politicians, central bank, and the overall banking system have created a HOUSE OF CARDS ready to collapse. This is why I do not believe most non-dividend paying equities (e.g., "growth stocks") are a particularly healthy way to speculate or "invest" (again, air quotes).

For those in the back: buying most of the popular (more well known) stocks in the stock market (and even diversified mutual funds) is NOT investing, but **speculation.** At worst, it is just gambling—pure and simple.

Our country's debt, inflation, and the various bubbles we're in (see Application: The Coming Storm), all paint a single picture: *collapse* (e.g., recession ... stagflation ... or even a depression). I don't want to be caught flat-footed if a major bust cycle happens, and it WILL happen; it's just a matter of WHEN.

Timing the marketplace is not something anyone can do well, so a sound investment and savings approach is one that weathers storms without causing you to lose your shirt. The pundits will say, "Well, you're giving up on huge potential returns by not being in the market."

Ramsey and other reckless financial advisers will often quote an "average of 10–12%+ return" when one keeps their money in the stock market. But they are not properly articulating (nor likely understanding) the sheer amount of risk being assumed given the current economic realities of rampant debt and the FED's interest rate and money supply manipulation.

Average Rate of Return vs. Real Return

My main objection with "average rate of return" statistics commonly cited when examining benefits of putting money in equity markets is that it is "technically accurate" but *factually inaccurate from an investment principle perspective.*

The average rate of return over a period does *not* measure the correct thing–in other words, the *RATE itself doesn't matter;* what matters is the impact on the **investment balance** during that same period of time (the ***"Real Return"***).

This is completely dependent on when you got in and the timing involved.

For example, assume someone told you they put $10,000 in the market and kept it there for 4 years (without investing another penny). They then said they made a -10% loss in year 1, +40% gain in year 2, -90% loss in year 3, and +125% gain in year 4.

The average return percentage over that period (4 years) is fairly easy to compute.

It's a **16.25%** average return at the end of four years. Nice!

That's a pretty awesome rate of return, right? 16.25% would be a great return to receive. However, consider what this means: it is NOT the *consistent* rate of return; it's the *average* rate of return.

This means some years were way down, and some were way up.

Standard (but flawed) logic people often use when investing money in the market long term is this: "There may be some up years, and down years, but overall, it'll all averages out to around 10–12% in the end."

Well, does it?

Let's now track the actual ending balance (after 4 years) of the $10K investment. Again, the math is fairly easy:

Year	Return	Loss/Gain	Balance
Year 0	(Initial Investment)	-	$10,000
Year 1	Loss of -10%. Boo!	-$1,000	$9,000
Year 2	Gain of +40%! Yay!	+$3,600	$12,600
Year 3	Loss of -90%! Yuck!	-$11,340	$1,260
Year 4	Gain of +125%! Amazing!	+$1,600	$2,835

This basic (albeit over-simplistic) example is very interesting. We can agree the AVERAGE rate of return over the 4 years was +16.25%. However, despite this, the investment of $10K dropped to just **$2,835** after the conclusion of 4 years.

The ACTUAL rate of return is a loss of **-72%!**

So average rates of return are quite telling—in how *little* they tell you.

They tell you *nothing* about how your investment will fair over a length of time.

The primary reason for this is simple: because the rate of return on risky investments like equities can often be *negative* in certain years (due to "busts" in the marketplace, aka "bear markets"), it can often take many years or even decades to recover!

Whoops, looks like you didn't time that well. (Hope you don't have to retire anytime soon ...)

But wouldn't it be better to deploy a large percentage of your money in a Tier 1 asset where the value of the asset can *only go UP and never go down?* How great would it be to experience the wonders of TRUE **uninterrupted compounding?**

And wouldn't it be terrific to be able to use that appreciating capital to consistently invest in far less risky **passive income streams?**

When preparing for retirement, wouldn't that be preferred...?

We'll examine this concept in depth in Chapter 5: Build Your Infinite Banking System. But, first, let's learn about why we must **Pay Ourselves First!**

In this chapter we learned the critical steps required to get out of debt and why it's crucial to avoid over-speculating in the stock market. Being able to do just these two things puts a **Warp Whistle** in your hands that catapults you directly to the magical world of saving and investing!

DID YOU KNOW?

The REAL rate of return of the S&P 500 over the last 30 years, when adjusted for inflation, is approximately 6.83%.

This rate of return reflects the actual purchasing power growth of an investment in the S&P 500 over that period.

And when one factors in a 15% capital gains tax rate, the 6.83% return further diminishes!

Think about the high risk taken by investors over those 30 years!

"So many of our dreams at first seem impossible, then they seem improbable, and then, when we summon the will, they soon become inevitable."

—Christopher Reeve

PLAYER 1
GIMME

CHEAT CODE #4

PAY YOURSELF FIRST

Written in 1926 *The Richest Man in Babylon* by George S. Clason is a timeless guide to personal finance, offering practical advice through engaging parables set in the ancient city of Babylon.

The book has resonated with both investors as well as everyday people for nearly a century because it presents foundational principles of wealth-building that are both simple and effective. One of the most significant lessons from the book is the concept of **Paying Yourself First,** a cornerstone of financial independence and long-term prosperity.

If you have children, I also *highly recommend* the accompanying illustrated children's series titled *The Richest Boy in Athens* authored by my good friend and business partner, Timothy F. Boyle. These books navigate the same key financial lessons shared by Clason but are beautifully illustrated and aimed at a younger audience.

Whether you're a seasoned financial pro or just getting started (or hoping to set your children up for long-term success), these secrets from ancient Babylon instill critical financial wisdom for creating value, saving money, living within your means, and judiciously investing capital.

The Richest Man in Babylon

The protagonist of the story's parables is a man named Arkad, who begins life as a poor scribe but eventually becomes the richest man in Babylon. His journey from poverty to wealth serves as a blueprint for anyone looking to improve their financial situation. Throughout the book, Arkad shares his wisdom with others, teaching them the principles that led to his success.

The Principle of "Paying Yourself First"

The concept of "paying yourself first" is central to the book's teachings. This principle suggests that *before* you pay any bills, purchase goods, or indulge in luxuries, you should first set aside a portion of your income for savings and investment. This portion is typically recommended to be at least 10% of your earnings. However, as you will see in Chapter 5: Build Your Infinite Banking System, the more you save ("capitalize your bank"), the more you can invest and build wealth! More on that later....

Regardless of the specific amount or exact percentage, the core concept remains the same: when you prioritize saving and investing as your foremost financial responsibility, you will always have the means to build wealth, regardless of your income level.

Arkad explains that the first step to accumulating wealth is to consistently save a portion of what you earn. By doing so, you not only create a habit of saving, but you also begin to build a foundation of capital that can be used for future investments. This savings, often referred to as the "seed" money, is crucial for generating passive income and growing your wealth over time.

Arkad's lesson is clear: even a modest income can lead to wealth if you are disciplined about saving. The principle of paying yourself first is about making your financial future a priority and ensuring that you have the resources to invest and grow your wealth.

Controlling Expenses

In addition to paying yourself first, the book emphasizes the importance of controlling expenses. Clason illustrates through the book's parables that many people, regardless of how much they earn, struggle financially because they allow their desires to outpace their income. The key takeaway: living within one's means is essential for financial stability!

Arkad advises against confusing desires with needs. While it is natural to want to enjoy the fruits of your labor, it is crucial to recognize that not all spending is necessary. By distinguishing between what is essential and what is merely a luxury, individuals can reduce unnecessary expenses and ensure that they have more money available to save and invest.

Clason shares a critical financial philosophy with Ramsey: the concept of **budgeting,** where you allocate your income to cover necessary expenses, save, and then spend on discretionary items.

This disciplined approach ensures that you live within your means and continuously grow your savings. By controlling your expenses, you create a surplus that can be directed toward wealth-building activities, rather than depleting your resources on fleeting pleasures.

Making Your Money Work for You

Another critical lesson from *The Richest Man in Babylon* is the importance of making your money work for you. Arkad emphasizes that once you have accumulated savings, the next step is to invest wisely.

The primary goal of investing is to generate **passive income** money that comes in regularly *without the need for continuous effort*. As you'll read later (Chapter 6: Create Passive Income Streams), Robert Kiyosaki's "Rich Dad" espouses this critical concept and makes it part of his financial philosophy.

Arkad likens money to workers who can earn income for you if properly employed. He advises investing in ventures that are secure and provide steady returns. For example, lending money at interest or investing in businesses that offer reliable dividends are ways to make your money work for you. The key is to ensure that your investments are sound and that you do not risk your principal on speculative ventures that promise high returns but carry significant risk.

The book warns against get-rich-quick schemes and emphasizes the importance of patience and prudence in investing. Arkad teaches that wealth is built over time through consistent, safe investments that gradually grow your capital. By reinvesting the returns from your investments, you can take advantage of the **compounding effect,** where your wealth grows exponentially.

Seek Wise Counsel and Continuous Learning

Arkad stresses the importance of seeking advice from those who are knowledgeable in financial matters. He encourages individuals to consult with experienced investors, bankers, and other experts before making investment decisions. This approach helps avoid costly mistakes and ensures that your money is invested wisely.

In addition to seeking counsel, Arkad advocates for continuous learning. The financial landscape is always changing, and staying informed is crucial for making smart investment decisions. Whether through books, seminars, mentorship, or investment guilds, ongoing education in finance is essential for maintaining and growing your wealth.

The Laws of Gold

The Richest Man in Babylon outlines several "laws of gold," that are essentially rules for wealth accumulation. These include:

- ☆ **Save a Portion of Your Income:** Consistently save at least 10%+ of what you earn to build a foundation for wealth.
- ☆ **Invest Wisely:** Put your savings to work by investing in secure opportunities that offer steady returns.
- ☆ **Avoid Risky Investments:** Be wary of speculating; don't invest much in assets you can't control, manage, or influence.
- ☆ **Seek Expert Advice:** Always consult with knowledgeable individuals before making financial decisions.
- ☆ **Protect Your Wealth:** Ensure that your investments are secure and that your wealth is protected from potential losses.

Actionable Advice

The Richest Man in Babylon provides a practical and timeless guide to wealth-building that remains relevant today. Its lessons are rooted in common sense and emphasize the importance of discipline, prudence, and financial education. By following the principle of **paying yourself first**, controlling expenses, and making wise investments, anyone can achieve financial independence and prosperity.

The book's teachings highlight that wealth is **not about how much you earn,** but rather about ***how much you keep and grow.***

By adopting the habits and mindset of the characters in Babylon, investors can take control of their financial future, build lasting wealth, and ultimately enjoy the security and freedom that comes with financial independence.

In the next chapter, you'll learn how to tie together the philosophy of "paying yourself first" with the Infinite Banking Concept (IBC)....

These two strategies, when bundled together, form a powerful NEW **Warp Whistle** that's perhaps the most powerful one in the entire financial game.

Combining these two into one creates a robust banking system—one far, far greater than the sum of its parts. *1 + 1 = 10!*

> *"The biggest risk of all is not taking one."*
> ***—Mellody Hobson***

IBC
BONUS!
PLAYER 1

CHEAT CODE #5

BUILD YOUR INFINITE BANKING SYSTEM

Nelson Nash's IBC Plan in a Nutshell

Everything from this chapter onward assumes you are out of debt (completed Baby Step #2 described in Chapter 3: Get Out of Debt) and that you have committed to "paying yourself first" (Chapter 4: Pay Yourself First).

I will now explain and attempt to distill the life-altering and powerful philosophy invented by Nelson Nash called the **Infinite Banking Concept** (or "IBC" for short).

It may sound complicated at first, but I promise it unlocks an invaluable **Warp Whistle** and investing power you cannot believe!

To conceptualize this premise, it's important to note that a person's need for a **stable and liquid means of banking** (by this I mean a way to quickly tap into funds for investments, large purchases, or emergencies) far exceeds any other financial requirement they have. It's drastically more important than their need for a high yield or investment return. A person's ability to access liquid funds is paramount!

The core concept here, before we get into the particulars, is understanding the purpose (goals / objectives) we are trying to accomplish. This is important before going forward:

1. **Better retirement planning** doesn't involve putting money in the "Wall Street Casino" (which is susceptible to booms and busts) but instead maintains safe and true uninterrupted compounding of the principal and interest.

2. **Access to capital** quickly for things like unplanned life events (weddings, funerals, medical issues, etc.) or, more ideally, opportune investment opportunities!
3. **Becoming your own banker** so you can benefit from the tremendous profits generated by the banking sector. Get involved in the banking business so you can pay yourself those gross banking profits instead.
4. **Removing yourself from the corrupt banking industry** (less important, but still a moral benefit) so that the inflation caused by fractional reserve banking, as perpetuated by the banking sector, is reduced.

Ok, so let's tackle these objectives one at a time. First, since I've already explained the hazards of the equity marketplace (see all previous chapters), let's continue the discussion by providing an alternative for where to put the bulk of retirement savings as well as liquid reserves to be used for making sound investment decisions.

Conventional wisdom continues to push equities hard because of the need to beat inflation. As an aside, inflation wouldn't be so high if Nixon hadn't gotten the USD off the gold standard and if the Federal Reserve ("the FED") did not continue to manipulate the money supply.

But that rabbit-hole aside (see Glossary for more context), the most conservative and traditional vehicle for saving money existed LONG before the stock market came into being.

It's the standard, plain, old, vanilla **Whole Life Insurance** product!

Whole Life Insurance Explained

Now, when most people think of life insurance, they don't think of savings or investing at all. Why would they? How can someone save money in their insurance policy? It's there as a last resort, not any sort of an asset, right?

Well, no, actually—not in this case.

When most people think of life insurance they think of term insurance (i.e., a fixed term/length of insurance, e.g., 20 years). Term life insurance functions the same way as other insurance, such as car insurance, fire insurance, etc. Both the insurance company (and you, the policyholder) are betting you never have to use it.

For example, if you pay for a 20-year term life policy when you're 30 years old, and you happen to die before you're 50, then your beneficiary(ies) get the slated death benefit defined by the policy. But if you don't die, then the insurance company gets to keep all the premiums you paid, and your beneficiaries don't receive a red cent.

Once the policy expires and you try to sign up for a subsequent 20-year term, it is understandably far more expensive. This is because the risk to the insurance company is greater because someone is more likely to die when they're older than when they're younger. Makes sense, right?

However, whole life insurance (aka "permanent life insurance") is different. As the moniker implies, it is for your WHOLE life. Thus, the insurance doesn't cancel, and rates don't increase after a certain period of time—even if you get terminal cancer, start smoking, take up spelunking, etc. The insurance company will pay a defined amount no matter what—either upon your death or when you reach age 121, whatever comes first. No other product is quite like this; because of that, whole life insurance is an asset you can use for banking!

Dividend-Paying Whole Life Insurance as a SAVINGS Vehicle

Since the beneficiaries of the insured (the person being covered by the policy) WILL be paid the death benefit at some point (i.e., everyone dies), the insurance company has a liability on their books. They have a contractual obligation to pay out the death benefit at some point, as long as the policy owner keeps paying the premium.

So, each premium payment made is building up **equity** in the policy!

This is a very important point, because this equity amount (just like a mortgage, for example) is getting closer and closer each month/year to being fully paid. And each year it collects interest on the cash deposits, plus any additional dividends.

The amount of equity in the insurance policy can NEVER go down or lose value—no matter what the market does. The dividends paid may fluctuate from year to year based on company performance, but the growth in the policy can only go *up*. As such, the asset **never breaks the compound interest curve!**

Tax Benefits of a Whole Life Policy

What's also worth noting is the tremendous tax advantages of the whole life instrument. It enjoys the same unique tax benefits as a **Roth IRA!** Since insurance premiums are paid post-tax, if you do it correctly, you'll *never have to pay tax on monies used from your banking system.* The appreciation in the policy is all tax-free. The policy loans taken are tax free. And ultimately the death benefit payout to your beneficiaries is tax free. You heard that right. When done right, any monies extracted from your banking system are 100% **not taxable!**

This makes IBC an incredible tool for retirement as well as a versatile banking system that can be used for investing.

This is especially true if you believe (as I do) that both capital gains tax as well as income tax rates in the U.S. will continue to *rise* due to our country's constant pull toward socialism.

I'll repeat for emphasis: *when you borrow from your policy(ies), using your cash value as collateral, this money will be completely and **100% tax-free!***

> **DID YOU KNOW?**
>
> To maximize efficiency, you will want to purchase life insurance policies from a mutual insurance company, which means the policyholders are the owners of the company.
>
> This is the best way to implement the IBC strategy, as it allows you to re-invest dividends into additional "paid up insurance," which will increase your cash value each year!

Dividend-Paying Whole Life Insurance as a BANKING Vehicle

A contractual feature you have as part of your policy is the ability to take out policy loans using the cash value you have accumulated in the policy. Remember: the policy is an asset on your "books" and a liability on the books of the insurance company. So, you can borrow against it, and the best (safest) thing the insurance company can do is make you a loan because it is fully insured by the collateral (the cash value).

An incredible feature about the nature of a policy loan is it isn't actually "coming out" of the policy itself—it's essentially a loan "on the side" while your principal continues to appreciate and gain in value due to interest and dividends!

Once again, **you never break the compound interest curve!!!**

A policy loan from an insurance company has no debt terms, no payment schedule, and no additional collateral (other than the cash value). What this means is you may choose NEVER to pay back the loan if you don't want to.

Unlike a conventional bank loan, there will be no lien against a physical asset like your house or your car when you purchase something with the loan. The insurance company won't even ask you what the loan is for—it's your money and you can do with it what you want, including not pay it back if you choose not to.

IBC Process in Greater Detail—Play "Honest Banker"

However, choosing not to pay back your policy loan(s) does not make you wealthier, as is the ultimate purpose. It may be a great "perk" of your policy contract, but Nelson Nash talks a great deal about playing "honest banker" with yourself.

He explains that when you practice IBC it means you take on another job and will always have two (2) jobs: your primary vocation (e.g., teacher, consultant, plumber, etc.) AND your second job: a banker.

It's this second job that allows you to collect interest and PAY YOURSELF what you might have paid the next best alternative (a bank) for a loan. Allow me to explain:

Let's say you purchase a $40,000/yr whole life insurance policy. This is now your "Bank."

You do this for six or seven years and accumulate (due to compounding interest and dividends accounted for) ~$290,000 in your cash value.

Now you need to purchase a new $50,000 truck. Okay, you have a few options.

1. You could pay cash (if you have it—but many people don't!). But, even if you do, the cash you're giving up on other things is its **opportunity cost**; meaning by paying cash you may give up the opportunity to make a lucrative $50k investment or other purchase.
2. You could take out a loan from a bank at 8.00% APR for 5 years (with the truck as the collateral). Or....
3. You could take a 5.50% policy loan from your whole life insurance policy—with no terms other than your promise (**to yourself**) to play honest banker.

Let's explore Option 3. If you take the loan out for $50,000 (at 5.5% payable to your insurance company), you should then come up with a plan to pay that loan back not at 5.5%, but at the higher rate you would have gotten with a bank loan—which was 8.00%.

In other words, you'll pay off the loan but intentionally pay MORE in interest. The difference you're paying (+2.5% APY each year) you're paying YOURSELF. You're "becoming your own banker" by paying yourself the difference in interest between what you should pay (but don't have to) and what you would have had to pay the bank if you didn't have a whole life policy at all.

DID YOU KNOW?

That additional 2.5% is being used to purchase additional insurance (these are called "*paid up additions*" or *PUAs* for short). They increase your cash value and improve the value of your Tier 1 asset (see Chapter 2)!

If you do this a few more times and follow this same process (e.g., for additional car purchases, annual business taxes, weddings, real estate purchases, etc.), the benefit will just keep getting better and better.

Your cash value will continue to rise as your "banking business" flourishes. You're investing all that extra money in yourself / your banking system. The more you borrow (and then pay back with the additional interest), the more your asset grows as the IBC process grows your Tier 1 liquid assets.

Ultimately, you'll have paid down your policy loan completely and can repeat the process all over again.

Capitalizing Your Bank

The above example was probably more to "nerd out" about the underlying process and demonstrate a mindset shift than it was to be practical for investing purposes. For, at the end of the day, *the purpose of having a well-funded IBC policy is NOT to buy liabilities* (cars, boats, etc.), but rather to purchase **INVESTMENTS.** Leveraging your bank to purchase cash flow-producing assets is precisely where the power of IBC becomes life changing!

Please allow me to clarify here that there is no "magic" to the Infinite Banking Concept. *It is not a financial panacea* that will solve all your problems. It is simply an instrument that allows the power of math (i.e., uninterrupted compounding and tax-free growth) to properly do its job—in a way no other asset can! However, it will take a great deal of time, diligence, patience, passion, and stick-with-it-ness to make IBC into a financial powerhouse for your needs and a storehouse for your wealth.

To that end, it's very important to note something that's critical. An IBC policy (or set of policies) MUST BE CAPITALIZED before it can be used. In other words, you must "seed it" like a garden. Money does not magically sprout out of the dirt once you own a properly structured whole life policy. It must be capitalized for many years in order to be useful!

For practical purposes, we also must understand that during the beginning years of an IBC policy, the Cash Value (CV), less your cumulative premium payments, will be negative. In other words, the total amount deposited into the policy (total premium payments) will be GREATER than the Cash Value ("CV") amount you have access to via policy loans for the first 5–7 years.

This is normal and expected! The reason for this is simply because the majority of the "administrative costs" of the whole life insurance are being paid up front during the first several years of the policy. And the policy will not "break even" until between year 4–7.

In his book *Becoming Your Own Banker*, Nelson Nash explains this process via an analogy. He states that if we were to start an actual brick-and-mortar bank, we'd have up front costs as well. We'd need to build the physical structure and pay for all the bureaucracy involved in opening a new bank. We'd have marketing expenses, legal fees, and costs for front-loading the bank's initial capital requirements, etc. In a way, the same thing happens with our **"IBC Bank."**

In fact, most of the administrative costs for the whole life policy are incurred during the *first two years.* That's just how it is. It's "the cost of doing business" in the banking industry, and you're a banker now! If you can wrap your head around that, you'll be fine. Because after those first 4–7 years ("the slow start"), the amazing growth process of an IBC policy starts snowballing quickly along an exponential growth curve!

As stated, around year 6 or 7 you will likely hit your **"Breakeven Point"** for the policy. This is when the CV (Cash Value) available in the policy **EXCEEDS** the total cumulative premiums deposited to date.

After this, the gravy train really kicks in. You've *capitalized your bank*! In fact, as the policy chugs along it only gets more and more "efficient." For example, by year 10, for each new $1.00 you deposit into the policy (via premiums), you can withdraw (through policy loans) **~$1.50!**

In other words, if a typical male aged 25 pays a premium of $5,000/mo ($60,000/yr) then in year 10 he will have access to an additional *$90,000* at the end of the year (that's **$30,000 MORE** than he paid in premiums that year)!

And it only gets better from there. By year 20, for every $1.00 he pays in premium, he gets access to an additional **$2.45 in CV!** Meaning that for the same exact $60,000 deposit (annual premium), he now has access to **$147,276!** Wow. *See Table on the following page representing a* ***REAL*** *policy illustration.*

That is the power of IBC!

Each and every year for the REST OF YOUR LIFE, that policy just gets more and more efficient. It allows each of your deposited dollars to multiply exponentially! This is one reason why IBC is perhaps the 11th miracle of the modern world!!

And what should you do with all those beautiful, manifested dollars each year? Yep, you guessed it: **invest them in cash flow-producing assets!**

"When you have a large amount of cash on hand all sorts of good opportunities will appear, and you can also negotiate very favorable purchase prices."
—Nelson Nash

Policy Illustration for Above Example (Consolidated)

Age	Cum. Annual Premium	Cash Value (CV)	$CV for $1 Prem	Death Benefit	Notes
26	$ 60,000	$ 45,697	$ 0.76	$ 2,135,898	Slow start year
27	$ 120,000	$ 96,452	$ 0.85	$ 2,347,142	Slow start year
28	$ 180,000	$ 151,199	$ 0.91	$ 2,558,493	Slow start year
29	$ 240,000	$ 215,464	$ 1.07	$ 2,770,070	CV delta breakeven
30	$ 300,000	$ 285,901	$ 1.17	$ 2,982,844	
31	$ 360,000	$ 358,073	$ 1.20	$ 3,195,347	
32	**$ 420,000**	**$ 434,335**	**$ 1.27**	**$ 3,408,556**	**Policy Breakeven**
33	$ 480,000	$ 514,837	$ 1.34	$ 3,622,665	
34	$ 540,000	$ 599,764	$ 1.42	$ 3,838,010	
35	$ 600,000	$ 689,319	**$ 1.49**	$ 4,054,784	**$1.49** for every $1 in prem (year 10)
36	$ 660,000	$ 783,316	$ 1.57	$ 4,273,304	
37	$ 720,000	$ 882,389	$ 1.65	$ 4,493,772	
38	$ 780,000	$ 986,793	$ 1.74	$ 4,716,567	
39	$ 840,000	$ 1,096,799	$ 1.83	$ 4,941,969	

Age	Cum. Annual Premium	Cash Value (CV)	$CV for $1 Prem	Death Benefit	Notes
40	$ 900,000	$ 1,212,724	$ 1.93	$ 5,170,279	
41	$ 960,000	$ 1,333,275	$ 2.01	$ 5,401,853	
42	$ 1,020,000	$ 1,460,129	$ 2.11	$ 5,636,800	
43	$ 1,080,000	$ 1,593,596	$ 2.22	$ 5,875,054	
44	$ 1,140,000	$ 1,734,233	$ 2.34	$ 6,116,580	
45	$ 1,200,000	$ 1,882,435	**$ 2.47**	$ 6,361,480	**$2.47** for every $1 in prem! (year 20)
46	$ 1,260,000	$ 2,038,635	$ 2.60	$ 6,609,949	
47	$ 1,320,000	$ 2,203,267	$ 2.74	$ 6,862,176	
48	$ 1,380,000	$ 2,376,669	$ 2.89	$ 7,118,078	
49	$ 1,440,000	$ 2,559,121	$ 3.04	$ 7,377,468	
50	$ 1,500,000	$ 2,751,169	$ 3.20	$ 7,640,359	
51	$ 1,560,000	$ 2,953,316	$ 3.37	$ 7,907,227	
52	$ 1,620,000	$ 3,166,243	$ 3.55	$ 8,178,734	
53	$ 1,680,000	$ 3,390,374	$ 3.74	$ 8,455,253	
54	$ 1,740,000	$ 3,626,302	$ 3.93	$ 8,737,073	
55	$ 1,800,000	$ 3,874,693	$ 4.14	$ 9,024,649	
56	$ 1,860,000	$ 4,136,368	$ 4.36	$ 9,318,628	
57	$ 1,920,000	$ 4,412,036	$ 4.59	$ 9,619,647	
58	$ 1,980,000	$ 4,702,469	$ 4.84	$ 9,928,258	
59	$ 2,040,000	$ 5,008,487	$ 5.10	$ 10,245,042	
60	$ 2,100,000	$ 5,330,867	**$ 5.37**	$ 10,570,674	**$5.37** for every $1 in premium!!!
61	$ 2,160,000	$ 5,670,386	$ 5.66	$ 10,905,778	

Removing Yourself from the Banking System

The tangential benefit of using the IBC process and becoming your own banker is that you'll have effectively (in all or in part) removed yourself from the banking system. Why is that important? Because the nature of the banking sector is morally corrupt in how it doles out loans.

For every single dollar ($1.00) a commercial bank takes in deposits, it is able to loan out ten dollars ($10.00) in loans. In this way it essentially creates new money out of thin air. Another word for this is **inflation**. The current banking system creates inflation.

This corrupt process is called "fractional reserve banking." Austrian Economists like Ludwik von Mises explained that this phenomenon (10:1 bank loans to bank reserves) is what helps contribute to the "boom/bust" cycle, aka "The Business Cycle."

In other words, the reason we tend to have 5–10 year "booms" in our economy and the stock market and then these giant CRASHES ("busts") is because of the business cycle, as perpetuated by fractional reserve banking as well as the Central Bank's manipulation of interest rates.

Disciples of the Austrian school of economics, like me, feel that the fractional reserve banking system is immoral, creates moral hazard, and thus any way to remove yourself from it is a positive thing. *Moral hazard* is simply a lack of incentive for guarding against risk when one feels they are (rightly or wrongly) fully insulated from its consequences.

For more information on this, please read the book *How Privatized Banking Really Works* by Carlos Lara and Dr. Robert Murphy (mentioned in the Introduction).

Investing with IBC vs. "Normal" Investing

So, what's the takeaway from all this? Well, simply stated, an IBC "Bank" can help function as another "financial cheat code"—**a Warp Whistle!**

When IBC is leveraged, it can propel an investor further than he ever could go using the standard/normal paradigms.

This flips conventional investing mantras on their head. For example, when considering an investment, most people spend the majority of their focus ("tunnel vision") analyzing only how to get the highest possible YIELD from the investment. Yield becomes the *be-all-end-all* metric of consideration. Nothing else matters but its yield (rate of return)!

As Nash posits in his book, an employee might gather around the water cooler at work with his colleagues to brag how he got a 10% APY return on his money in this-or-that stock. Or maybe he even got a 20% return! Hell, maybe his money doubled!

Big whoop! Why? Because think about it this way—the money that was invested by the employee represents just a **tiny fraction** of his total pool of capital. It's the "fun money" he used only AFTER he has paid all his bills and his taxes and all his household expenses.

Normal Dave Chases Yield and Speculates

For example, let's assume this person (we'll call him "Normal Dave") makes $150,000/yr as his annual salary. After 34.1% of his salary is stolen by the federal government via taxes (NB: his BIGGEST expense by the way—more on that later in Chapter 8: Legally Avoid Taxes), his take-home pay is reduced to $98,826/yr. That equates to $8,235.50/mo.

So, consider this very realistic breakdown of Normal Dave's financials:

- ☆ Dave read Chapter 4 and is smart enough to save 10% of his salary, $823.55/mo (leaving $7,411.95/mo)
- ☆ Dave's mortgage is $3,000/mo (leaving $4,411.95/mo)
- ☆ His utilities sum to $850/mo (leaving $3,561.95/mo)
- ☆ His car payment is $400/mo (leaving $3,161.95/mo)
- ☆ His family's grocery bill is $750/mo (leaving $2,411.95/mo)
- ☆ His property taxes are $8,500/yr, or $708.33/mo (leaving $1,703.62/mo)
- ☆ His kid's school supplies, sports, and extracurriculars are $100/mo (leaving $1,603.62/mo)
- ☆ His average discretionary budget for items like restaurants (eating out) and entertainment/movies is $500/mo (leaving $1,103.62/mo)
- ☆ His average debt payment for college loans and credit cards is $300/mo (leaving $803.62/mo)
- ☆ So, Dave's TOTAL expense spending per month is $6,608.33/mo
- ☆ And, after saving $823.55/mo, he has roughly $1,627.17/mo left over to do with as he pleases.

I feel the numbers above are quite conservative. They don't even bake into the equation the miscellaneous "break/fix" scenarios that routinely come up for household or vehicle repairs, etc. But let's give our friend Dave every benefit of the doubt and say that of the $1,627.17 available after paying all his expenses, he chooses to put **$1,000.00/mo** into the stock market.

After paying all your expenses, if you can only safely invest $1,000/mo, you for damn sure want to make every penny invested receive the highest possible return, right?

So ... **Dave chases yield!** He speculates.

Dave puts his leftover cash "into the market" and chases that "hot lead" his friend at work told him about regarding some startup company or a hot stock like NVIDIA, AMC, Gamestop, or Shopify. Dave perhaps grabs some sweet Bitcoin while he's investing in exciting tech stocks—as he hears people are making money hand-over-fist in crypto, too!

Normal Dave then signs up for and reads "hot tips" and articles from all the best financial websites like The Motley Fool; he obsessively checks his stock market app—often hourly. And Dave waits diligently for his moonshot....

Even if Dave wasn't super aggressive—let's say he decided to invest in the (safer) "blue chips,"—he's not likely receiving a consistent stock dividend and instead is hoping and praying for significant appreciation on his stock purchases. He has little to no control, collateral, or flexibility. Therefore, he's not investing; he's ***speculating.***

But—let's examine what Dave has really done. He's effectively taken the balance of what he had **LEFT OVER** after all his expenses were paid and then put the remainder (his "fun money") into the market to chase yield.

So EVEN if he gets the "moonshot" he hoped would come, he has only speculated (at most) $1,000.00/mo into equities. We can't fault him; you saw his budget above—that's all he had, right?

Thus, when Dave meets his colleagues at the water cooler after a few weeks and his stocks are up 10%, he feels pretty darn good about himself!

Of course, he put his entire principal at risk (he could have lost 30–50% or more of his money). But ... things are good now. He's up 10%!

Yet ... let's examine this a bit deeper. What did Normal Dave really gain?

- In the first year he risks $1,000.00 each month to achieve a capital gain of $670.28 (10% APY, 0.83% per month) for the first $12,000 he invests.
- When one calculate capital gains taxes (-15%), he's actually booked a **$569.74 gain.**

As the years proceed on, compound growth does its magic. But to be clear: Dave takes on a lot of risk, but the returns are relatively unimpressive because the total volume of invested funds are paltry.

That's not his fault, though! It's not Normal Dave's fault he can't invest too much; he has a family and bills and a house to pay for!

However, let's take this just one or two steps further.

Let's actually give Dave the absolute *rosiest* of all possible outlooks. Let's assume his portfolio continues to track UP by 10% APY (+0.83%/mo) every single month for 84 months straight (7 full years) *without exception!*

Even with this most sanguine (and frankly unrealistic) scenario, the most Dave could make on his $1,000.00/mo speculation into the stock market for 7 years is a gain of $37,958.34 (that's net gain above his principal).

Oh, and guess what? Once again, the capital gains on that profit are fully TAXABLE when he decides to sell. The government demands its chunk of flesh, after all. It has unconstitutional wars to wage!

So, take away long-term capital gains tax (-15%) and Dave now has a total net gain of $32,264.59. And if you throw in just one bad year in the mix (far more likely given the nature of stock market ups-and-downs), you can **cut those returns by half** or more!

In fact, running the numbers reveals a disturbing truth: if Normal Dave had just two (2) really poor MONTHS at the tail end of 7 consecutive years of 10% positive growth (representing some sort of market crash or correction), he would likely face a net LOSS on his entire investment despite the preceding 7 excellent growth years! Specifically, it would take just two (2) back-to-back -16.40% months to wipe out his **entire $37.95K** pre-tax gain! Now, that's humbling to think about.

At the end of the day, Normal Dave was so focused on chasing the **YIELD** for his meager investment (yield is a beautiful siren's song for speculators!) that he missed a far better way: to consider instead the **VOLUME** of money he might enable to flow into his own banking system and achieve uninterrupted compound growth!

So, let's consider an alternative approach to what the "Normal" people like Dave routinely do....

"Extraordinary Jonathan" Capitalizes His Bank and Invests

Instead of putting the paltry amount of money that is left over after Dave paid all his bills and expenses, what if someone did it the "IBC Way?" How would that impact the numbers?

For example, consider this outrageous idea. What would happen if someone ran some, most, or maybe even their ENTIRE paycheck through their banking system?

Now, instead of worrying about what investment YIELD was being made on the "cherry" left over after all one's expenses were paid, they instead were able to attain uninterrupted compounding and tax-free appreciation on the ENTIRE CAKE!

With respect to the original salary figures, let's re-run the numbers with a new bloke named "Extraordinary Jonathan."

Jon works beside "Normal Dave," and they have the exact same salary; and, as luck would have it, they also have the EXACT same monthly expenses. What are the chances!

- ☆ $150K salary less taxes = **$98,826/yr.** That's $8,235.50/mo.
  - Note: W2 salary employees can do little about their tax burden. But don't worry—there is a TON to talk about on that front as we get into Chapters 6 and 7!

- ☆ Jon opens a properly designed IBC policy and deposits **$5,000/mo** of his $8,235/mo salary as premium.
    - Some experts refer to this action as "Forced Savings;" as just the psychological impact of taking this one step works wonders on your financial picture (see Chapter 4: Pay Yourself First). But that's not the point of this exercise. The numbers are what really matter; so, let's keep going....
- ☆ Jon pays what household expenses he can from the remaining $3,235.50/mo and then takes a POLICY LOAN for the difference of **$3,373.33/mo**, (NB: this takes **nothing** "out" of his policy; it does not touch the principal! Jon is simply taking a loan "on the side" from the insurance company and collateralizing the policy's cash value.)
- ☆ The $5,000/mo ($60k/yr) premium appreciates tax-free due to dividends and the guaranteed rate of return within the policy.
- ☆ After 7 years the $5,000/mo premiums create an asset worth **~$431,976.**
    - This is more than his cumulative premiums deposited by ~$11.9K.
    - NB: Again, for a properly-designed IBC policy, its "break-even point" is somewhere between years 4 and 7.
- ☆ When you take into consideration Jon's policy loans, totaling to $344,684.81 (which have accumulated in order to pay **$3,373.33/mo** of his monthly expenses @ 5.50% interest), it makes Jon's accessible Cash Value (CV) the difference between those two values: $432K–$344.7K = **$87.3K** (this figure represents the *extra money* Jon earned doing nothing different from Dave other than building his "IBC Banking System").
    - NB: Jon, by virtue of simply following the IBC process of funding a policy and taking policy loans to pay for a portion of his monthly expenses, has ironically already created more of a return than Normal Dave did by speculating in the stock market ($32.2K). This is because Jon focused on the **VOLUME** of money through his banking system, allowing uninterrupted, tax-free, and RISK-FREE compounding to work to his advantage.
- ☆ *BUT it gets better!* So far this is just window-dressing. We're just getting warmed up....

- ☆ Jon is savvy and decides to follow the advice outlined in subsequent chapters (we'll get to them soon enough) and buy a **cash flow-producing asset.** He buys, for example, a real estate property and puts down $75,000 as a down payment!
  - To fund this purchase, he takes a policy loan (from his $87.3K CV) for $75K and buys the property!
- ☆ In short order, that property soon begins to cash flow $2,000/mo.
- ☆ Jon read Nelson Nash's book, so, he plays "honest banker" and uses the $2,000/mo from the rental income to pay down the policy loan of $75,000; doing this, he pays back the policy loan in just over 3 years.

Extraordinary Jon now has the following assets that Dave does not:

- ☆ Over $100K in CV in his life insurance (which will continue to grow each and every month), to be used on other investments.
- ☆ A death benefit (this is an extra perk, not the point of IBC).
- ☆ A real estate asset paying $2,000/mo in passive income each month.

Extraordinary Jon is now in a MUCH better financial position after just ten years than Normal Dave.

And why should Jon not "rinse and repeat" and do this strategy over and over and over and over again?

The contrast between Normal Dave and Extraordinary Jon is extreme. They are now on VERY different financial paths.

HINT

It was a trick question; he should!

If Jon continues to fund his (now very efficient) IBC policy and use the cash value (CV) to purchase real estate just three or four more times, he'll soon reach financial freedom!

He will be able to quit his job, because his **Personal Income will be greater than his Monthly Expenses ("PI > ME")** (See Chapter 6).

That's the power of IBC and passive investing! Dave may be in the "rat race" for the rest of his life—chasing yield with every mediocre hand he plays at the

"Wall Street Casino"—using only the money he occasionally has left over after paying all his bills.

Even IF Dave is wildly lucky (and most people aren't—remember, it's called the "Wall Street Casino" for a reason) and he beats all the odds, the most he can hope for is being able to buy a new car or vacation with his occasional stock market winnings.

Dave Isn't Building Generational Wealth.

Dave isn't funding his own **bank**. He isn't buying **cash flow-producing assets**. He *isn't gaining control over his future.*

In fact, Dave isn't **investing** at all; he is **speculating** with "play money" left over after the mountain of bills on his desk have been paid.

In terms of risk, Extraordinary Jon also wins out! Using his **IBC Bank** and purchasing cash flow-producing passive assets (see Chapter 6) turns out to be far **LESS RISKY** than trying to "chase yield" in risky markets.

In short, Normal Dave felt he had to be riskier to get a higher return, but the ***exact opposite turned out to be true.***

DID YOU KNOW?

The insurance company making a policy loan to the policyholder is the *safest* bet the insurance company can possibly make!

The cash value collateralizes the loan. So even if the policyholder never pays back a dime of principal, the insurance company simply will get its full payment due at the time of death.

It's 100% guaranteed the insurance company will be paid in full—they'll just subtract the balance of the loan from the death benefit when they pay it.

This creates a WIN/WIN between the policyholder and insurance company.

See the breakdown in the following chart:

	TOOLSET	MINDSET	RISK	ASSET CONTROL	RETURNS
Normal Dave **(Speculating)**	Stock Market	Scarcity Mindset	**HIGH**	**NONE**	**LOW**
Extraordinary Jonathan **(Investing)**	IBC Banking, Uninterrupted Compounding, Cash flow-Producing Passive Assets	Abundance Mindset	**LOW**	**HIGH**	**HIGH**

Powerful Closing Thoughts

Hopefully this simple example outlines the power of capitalizing one's BANK and also why one's need for liquidity, control, flexibility, and interrupted compounding far, far exceeds his need to receive a high yield.

The "normal" philosophy employed by Dave—chasing yield with the paltry funds he had left over—exhibits a "scarcity mindset." He is trying to do a lot with a little.

The "Extraordinary" philosophy employed by Jonathan focused instead on the **VOLUME** of money he could put through his bank. He gained the power of **uninterrupted compounding** and **tax-free growth** to seed his bank for several years, and then used those funds to invest in **cash flow-producing assets.** This exhibits an "abundance mindset."

Jon picked up the **Warp Whistle** of the Infinite Banking Concept (IBC) and was able to accomplish infinitely more than Dave. The joyful tune an IBC "Whistle" can play is a beautiful and inspiring song. It will take you further in the game than you ever imagined possible.

Recapping the Value of the Infinite Banking Concept

If I've done a halfway decent job in the preceding pages, then you should be walking away with the following takeaways:

1. What IBC Is and What It's Not:

- ☆ ***Infinite Banking is NOT an investment;* your whole life policy is NOT an investment**
- ☆ Infinite Banking is NOT about the *rate of return* of an investment.
- ☆ Infinite Banking IS an incredibly powerful tool for **FINANCING** investments you choose to make.

2. IBC Provides Guaranteed Growth

- ☆ The underlying value in your IBC policy/polices can **NEVER GO DOWN**; it will only go up.
- ☆ Infinite Banking takes advantage of the magic of **uninterrupted compounding.** You never break the compound interest curve.
- ☆ Whole life policies have two growth components: (1) a **guaranteed rate of return** as well as (2) a **dividend payment.**
    1. CV grows at a *guaranteed rate*, regardless of market fluctuations. This provides stability and predictability, unlike investments tied to stocks or other volatile markets.
    2. Dividends can (and should) be reinvested into the policy to further boost cash value and the death benefit. Dividends can be used to increase policy growth or even to reduce premium payments.
- ☆ Always choose to work with a MUTUAL life insurance company that has consistently paid dividends for 175+ years. Examples include *Northwestern Mutual, Penn Mutual, MassMutual*, and *New York Life.*
- ☆ NB: Ignore the little devil on your left shoulder telling you "*... but I can get a higher return elsewhere!*"
    - IBC is not about yield; it's about **VOLUME.**

- IBC is an **"*AND* asset"**; it is not something you do at the expense of doing something else. IBC is a framework you use *FOR* investing. It fuels and turbo-charges your investment approach. For example:

  IBC ***AND*** Real Estate investing ...

  IBC ***AND*** Funding/Creating a Business ...

  IBC ***AND*** Personal Lending ...

3. IBC Provides Tax-Free Growth

- ☆ When used correctly, all monies from your Bank (e.g., "withdrawals" via policy loans as well as appreciation of the asset via dividends and the guaranteed rate of return) are **100% TAX-FREE!**
- ☆ To clarify, the cash value of a whole life insurance policy technically grows *tax-deferred*, meaning you do not pay taxes on appreciation as the principle grows. However, taking out policy loans (vs. making withdrawls) to access the CV ensures you will *never pay a dime in taxes!*
- ☆ Again, **policy loans are not taxed;** the death benefit is also paid out **tax-free** to beneficiaries.

4. IBC Provides Control and Flexibility

- ☆ With funds in your IBC Bank, you maintain **complete control** of your capital!
- ☆ There are **flexible repayment terms** for loans against policies (i.e., you set the terms!).

5. Additional Perks of IBC

- ☆ Whole life insurance (in many states) is completely **protected from creditors.** Divorce? Lawsuit? This asset can't be touched!
- ☆ IBC + Passive Investing allows you to build **generational wealth!**

6. IBC Guiding Principles and Best Practices:

- ☆ Don't chase yield with the meager amount of money you have leftover after paying all your bills! Instead focus on the VOLUME of money going into your Infinite Banking System.

- ☆ Your pool of available cash needs to reside somewhere (e.g., a savings account, checking account, IRA, etc.). A well-structured IBC Banking System is the BEST place to maintain your capital.
    - Make your IBC Bank the "**storehouse of your wealth.**"
- ☆ Play "Honest Banker" with yourself (i.e., "don't steal the peas," as Nelson Nash explains in his book *Becoming Your Own Banker*—go read it!)

Put the Principles All Together!

As you hopefully are seeing, you can (and should) start to combine the myriad principles described in this book and use them in tandem!

You'll understand the proper asset allocations described by the Wealth Pyramid (Chapter 2) and quickly **Debt Snowball** your way out of debt (Chapter 3). You'll focus on **Paying Yourself First** (Chapter 4) by opening a whole life insurance policy. Over time you will capitalize your **IBC Bank** (Chapter 5) so you can ultimately deploy your liquid Tier 1 capital from your bank and invest it in passive **Cash Flow-Producing Assets** (Chapter 6).

Do you now see how all the pieces start to fit together??

Following this system is not just exciting; it will bring financial freedom!

But let's dive deep into the fun investment stuff a bit more! In the next chapter we will learn how to **Create Passive Income Streams** and exactly how to make one's **P**assive **I**ncome exceed their **M**onthly **E**xpenses **(PI > ME).** For once we've done that, we've blown the last **Warp Whistle,** beaten King Bowser, quit our job forever, and won the game....

"The common man has become so infatuated with living for today that the importance of saving—of creating capital—is all but a lost value."

—Nelson Nash

PLAYER 1
FOR SALE
SOLD!

CHEAT CODE #6

CREATE PASSIVE INCOME STREAMS (PI > ME)

Okay, so now you have established how to build your **bank** (Chapter 5) in which to store Tier 1 capital. However, this capital must then be used to make sound investments by purchasing **cash flow-producing assets.**

We're really jumping those game levels now! We just warped from Level 2 to Level 8 in a single puff of that magical Whistle. It's a BIG step to begin the process of capitalizing your **IBC Bank.** Very few are this motivated or passionate about their financial future. This makes you weird. This makes you extraordinary!

But having your IBC Bank is just the first step. It's not just a matter of having your bank; it's *using* your bank that counts.

This may remind you of the *Seinfeld* episode in which Jerry goes to the teller of the car rental agency to explain he has a reservation for a vehicle. Unfortunately, there is no car for him; they've all been rented. He points out that they TOOK his reservation but didn't HOLD it. As he explains to the teller (with flourishing arm-waving and bravado).

> "You see, you know how to *take* the reservation, you just don't know how to *hold* the reservation. And that's really the most important part of the reservation: the *holding*. Anybody can just take them...."

It's the same with Infinite Banking (kind of); you now know how to *create* your Bank. Yet now you need to learn how to *USE* your bank. Because that's really the most important part of the Bank: *using it!*

The previous chapter provided the framework in which to build a solid foundation for success. Your bank is your *system*; but IBC is just your VEHICLE for success; you still need to learn how to drive.

So, please take note–IBC is simply "the means" to "the end." The "means" of this strategy effectively creates for you an investing launch pad for obtaining "the end": **cash flow-producing investments.**

In other words, practicing IBC is NOT investing. Rather, IBC better enables investing. IBC allows you the ability to more easily invest capital from your Bank into **cash-flowing assets!**

You may decide to start your own business! You may decide to invest in real estate. You may decide to pursue opening a franchise or place ATMs around your town. You may decide to invest in a managed fund or offer private/personal lending to friends and family. There are now a MILLION options open to you. With access to cash comes *opportunity*!

So, that being said, let's dive into the wide world of the financial genius Robert Kiyosaki. He literally "wrote the book," so to speak, on both how to think about passive investing and also how to do it!

Rich Dad, Poor Dad

No single book has had a more profound impact on my life than Robert Kiyosaki's *Rich Dad, Poor Dad*. It is a game-changer.

Within the pages of his chef-d'oeuvre, Kiyosaki provides a unique perspective on wealth-building, contrasting the financial philosophies of two father figures in his life: his own biological father ("Poor Dad") and the father of his best friend ("Rich Dad").

The book emphasizes the importance of financial education, the mindset needed to achieve financial freedom, and strategies for building wealth through passive income.

Eventually (spoiler alert) he comes to realize that his "Rich Dad" gave him far better financial advice because the "normal" advice of his "Poor Dad" would have set him on a path to financial mediocracy.

The ultimate lesson he teaches is the need for investors to build **passive investments,** with the ultimate goal of escaping the "rat race" (i.e., achieving financial freedom), which he defines as when one's Passive Income exceeds their Monthly Expenses **(PI > ME).**

The Two Dads and Their Financial Philosophies

Kiyosaki's biological father, whom he refers to as "Poor Dad," was a well-educated man with a stable job in the government. He believed in the traditional path of working hard, getting a good education, and securing a stable job. Despite his high educational achievements, Poor Dad struggled financially, living paycheck to paycheck and eventually dying in debt.

In contrast, "Rich Dad" was his best friend's father, who did not have a formal education but was a successful entrepreneur and investor. Rich Dad believed in the importance of financial education, investing in assets, and making *money work for you* rather than *working for money.*

This distinction between working for money (earned income) and having money work for you (passive income) is central to Kiyosaki's philosophy. He said repeatedly "the rich don't work for their money. Their money works for them."

Assets vs. Liabilities

Another core principle in Kiyosaki's body of work is understanding the difference between **assets** and **liabilities**.

Assets are things that *put money into your pocket*, while liabilities are things that *take money out of your pocket*. This definition is crucial because it bucks "normal" and challenges conventional wisdom, which often considers things like a personal home as an asset.

So, unless your home generates income (such as through STR income), it is ***NOT an asset but a liability*** because it incurs costs. To achieve PI > ME, an investor must consider assets that generate **passive income.**

These assets often include:

- ☆ **Real Estate:** Rental properties that provide steady income streams.
- ☆ **Dividend-Paying Stocks and Bonds:** Investments that can yield dividends or interest over time.
- ☆ **Businesses:** Owning or investing in businesses that generate profits without your direct involvement.
- ☆ **Intellectual Property:** Royalties from books, music, patents, or other activities.

DID YOU KNOW?

The best way to turn a significant liability, one's primary residence, into an asset is to rent it out on short-term rental marketplaces like Airbnb and VRBO!

This will require a bit more insurance and some logistical planning (lock up the valuables!), but the effort is well worth it.

You'll also be able to write off a pro rata portion of household expenses related to the upkeep of the house (including utilities, repairs, etc.) against the income you make on the rental!

The Importance of Financial Education

Kiyosaki also stresses that financial education is the foundation of wealth-building. The traditional education system teaches people how to work for money but not how to make money work for them. Financial literacy involves understanding how money works, how to manage it, and how to invest it wisely.

"Rich Dad" taught Robert to read financial statements, understand the tax code, and recognize opportunities for investing in assets. This knowledge enables individuals to make informed decisions that can lead to financial independence. Without financial education, even those with high incomes can end up in financial distress if they do not know how to manage their money effectively.

Building Passive Income Streams

Once again, the cornerstone of Kiyosaki's investing philosophy is building **passive income streams.** Passive income is money earned with little to no effort on the part of the investor. Unlike earned income, which requires continuous effort and time (like a W2 job), passive income continues to flow even when the individual is not actively working.

To attain passive income, one must **acquire cash flow-producing assets.** Invest in assets that fit with your interests and passions. Your passive income will grow with each cash flow-producing asset acquired. Financial freedom is achieved when one's passive income exceeds their Monthly Expenses (PI > ME).

Once you have achieved this milestone, you no longer need to work! Your assets are doing the work for you. What's more, you have created generational wealth and exited the "rat race."

Steps to Building Passive Income

1. **Invest in Income-Generating Assets**
   - ☆ Start by identifying and investing in assets that produce stable, recurring, passive income. This could be real estate, managed funds, or businesses.
   - ☆ The key is to ensure that these investments require minimal ongoing effort to maintain.
2. **Reinvest Earnings**
   - ☆ Reinvest the income generated from your assets back into acquiring more assets. In other words: **rinse and repeat.** This creates a compounding effect, where your wealth grows exponentially over time because your cash flow-producing assets are growing.
3. **Minimize Liabilities**
   - ☆ Avoid accumulating liabilities that drain your finances. This includes unnecessary debt, expensive consumer goods, and other expenditures that do not generate income.
   - ☆ Live below your means and direct excess income toward investments. Flow deals through your IBC policy(ies).

4. **Leverage and Debt**

    - ☆ While Kiyosaki strongly warns against "bad debt" (debt used to purchase liabilities), he is a proponent of using "good debt" (used to acquire income-generating assets).
    - ☆ For example, taking a mortgage to purchase a rental property can be a strategic move if the rental income exceeds the mortgage payments and other costs.

5. **Focus on Cash Flow**

    - ☆ Cash flow is the lifeblood of financial freedom. The amount of cash flow from your assets, not their total value, determines your financial independence.
    - ☆ A high-value asset that does not generate cash flow is less useful than a lower-value asset that does!

Achieving Financial Independence

Again, financial independence (aka "financial freedom") is only achieved when one's Passive Income exceeds their Monthly Expenses.

Financial Freedom = PI > ME

Once achieved, you are no longer dependent on a job or active work to maintain your lifestyle. Kiyosaki calls this "getting out of the rat race," which is when you escape the cycle of working hard to pay bills and instead live off the income generated by your assets.

The Process of Achieving Financial Independence:

1. **Set Clear Financial Goals**

    - ☆ Set specific, measurable financial goals. Determine how much passive income you need to cover your monthly expenses and set a timeline for achieving this goal.

2. Create a Budget and Track Expenses

- ☆ Understanding your monthly expenses is crucial. Create a budget that outlines your essential expenses and discretionary spending. By tracking your expenses, you can identify areas where you can cut costs and redirect those savings into investments.
- ☆ You might note (if you're paying attention) that this is THIRD time this concept has been mentioned in this book. The critical importance of active budgeting was outlined earlier by the works of Clason, Ramsey, and Nash. *Sensing a theme here?*

3. Increase Your Income Streams and Reduce Your Risk

- ☆ Diversify your sources of passive income. Relying on a single income stream can be risky, so attempt to create *multiple streams* from different types of assets. This could include a combination of rental properties, dividend stocks, funds, and business income.
- ☆ Speaking for myself, certain people often used to ask me when I quit my job if I was scared to not have a "stable income" anymore. They felt I was being risky by not being a W2 employee. I typically replied: "You're the one taking a big risk; not me. You have ONE client. I have many. If your employer (your only 'client') ever fires you, you're unemployed. All your eggs are in that one basket! However, if a client fires me, I have 200 more to take their place. ***I am taking far less risk than you***...."

4. Continuously Educate Yourself

- ☆ The financial world is constantly changing, so continuous learning is essential. Read books, attend seminars, and seek advice from mentors and colleagues who are experienced in wealth-building.
- ☆ Staying informed allows you to adapt to new opportunities and challenges in the market.

5. Take Calculated Risks

- ☆ Investing always involves risk, but educated, *calculated risks* are necessary for financial growth.
- ☆ Step out of your comfort zone, try new investment strategies, and learn from both successes and failures.

6. **Be Patient and Persistent**

- ☆ Achieving financial independence is not an overnight process.
- ☆ Building a solid portfolio of income-generating assets takes time, and there will be setbacks along the way.
- ☆ However, staying focused on your long-term goals will ultimately lead to success.

The Mindset Shift

A significant component of financially successful people is the **mindset shift** required to build wealth.

Most people are trapped in a *scarcity mindset*, where they believe that money is limited and hard to come by. This mindset leads to fear-based financial decisions, such as avoiding risks and sticking to a traditional job for security.

"Rich Dad," on the other hand, had an *abundance mindset*. He believed that money is abundant and that opportunities for wealth are everywhere if you know where to look. This mindset encourages taking risks, investing in oneself, and seeking out new opportunities.

It is important to adopt the mindset of an **investor** rather than a consumer.

Consumers focus on spending money on liabilities that depreciate in value, while investors focus on **acquiring assets** that appreciate or generate income. This shift in mindset is crucial for building passive income and achieving financial independence.

Passive Investment Leads to Generational Wealth

Lastly, you'll find as you invest your wealth in cash-flowing assets, you are now creating **generational wealth** for you and your family.

Take a moment to think about the many differences in strategy and outcome between a) creating passive cash flow from assets and b) building a nest egg for retirement in a qualified plan like a 401(k).

In the latter, the investor is risking much to build up a pool of funds for their golden years. When retirement arrives, they HOPE they can live off their 401(k) long enough so that it lasts until they die. That's a **scarcity mindset**. They can only pray they die before the funds dry up! Maybe if they're "lucky" they'll die with enough money left over to give some sort of an inheritance to their children. This is hardly generational wealth!

The alternative strategy of owning cash flow-producing assets ensures stability and a quality of life that lasts in perpetuity and can be handed down to children and their children after them! That's an **abundance mindset.**

Another truth about this strategy is this: *opportunities find cash.*

Assuming you have established a robust bank (see Chapter 5: Build Your Infinite Banking System), you will soon be able to locate PASSIVE ways to create cash flow by buying assets—these are the ones which will serve you best in "retirement" (if you believe in such a term).

But, either way, creating a system of cash flow-producing assets will allow you to find and blow into a **Warp Whistle** which places you miles ahead of your peers who are shoving away dollars into a 30–50 year monetary prison called 401(k) or some other government-sponsored qualified plan.

Don't jump off a cliff just because your friends and peers do! **Seek alternative strategies.**

Grow your wealth and start "banking" on yourself.

I grow generational wealth by investing in cash flow-producing assets, not mindlessly hoping a pot of gold will be there for you at the end of the rainbow (the "normal" 401k/403b strategy).

Take charge of your OWN financial success; don't rely on the stock market to do it for you. And don't expect the government to assist, support, equip—and certainly not to save you in your golden years.

Remember: Financial Freedom = PI > ME

Creating Passive Income that exceeds your Monthly Expenses (PI > ME) is the name of the game.

Work furiously at this goal! Don't let it out of your sight. I will repeat myself. Once your PI > ME, you've blown all the Warp Whistles and "won" the financial game of life. You've achieved financial freedom, escaped the rat race, and can quit your full-time job (if you want to).

"If you don't find a way to make money while you sleep, you will work until you die."

—Warren Buffett

LEVEL UP!
PLAYER 1

CHEAT CODE #7

MOVE TO THE RIGHT SIDE OF THE QUADRANT

I guess before starting this chapter, I should probably explain what the *Cash Flow Quadrant* is. Well, once again we must dip into the deep pool of wisdom from our *Rich Dad, Poor Dad* financial guru, Robert Kiyosaki.

In his follow-up work, *The Cash Flow Quadrant*, he differentiates how the rich use their time and resources from how the poor and middle class use their time and resources.

The Cash Flow Quadrant

To visualize the distinction, Kiyosaki introduces the concept of the **Cash Flow Quadrant,** a tool that categorizes individuals into *four different types* based on how they generate income.

E	B
Employees	Business Owners
S	**I**
Self-Employed	Investors

Those on the "Left" trade time for money (e.g., those working for an employer or for themselves); those on the "Right" allow money to make them more money. The methods people earn money impact their financial independence and wealth-building potential.

Quadrant Breakdown

Each quadrant has very specific characteristics and mindsets: Those on the LEFT trade time for money; those on the RIGHT have their *money* or *systems* make them money.

1. **E–Employee:** *LEFT SIDE OF QUADRANT*

   - ☆ **Characteristics:** Employees work for someone else and earn money through a salary or hourly wage. They *trade time for money* and often seek job security, benefits, and a steady paycheck.

   - ☆ **Mindset:** Employees typically prioritize stability and security over financial risk. However, they are often limited in their earning potential because they can only work so many hours in a day.

2. **S–Self-Employed:** *LEFT SIDE OF QUADRANT*

   - ☆ **Characteristics:** Self-employed individuals own their jobs. They work for themselves and are often professionals like marketing consultants, doctors, lawyers, or small business owners. They have more control than employees but *still trade time for money*. In fact, very often they are working MORE hours than an ***E*** (e.g., 60+ hours a week) but because they "work for themselves" they rationalize the pain.

   - ☆ **Mindset:** The self-employed value independence and control but often struggle with work-life balance. Their income is directly tied to their effort, meaning they must work hard to earn more.

3. **B–Business Owner:** *RIGHT SIDE OF QUADRANT*

   - ☆ **Characteristics:** Business owners own a *system* or a business that works for them. They leverage other people's time, skills, and money to generate income. Unlike the self-employed, business owners do not need to be involved in every aspect of the business for it to generate income.

   - ☆ **Mindset:** Business owners focus on building systems that generate income, even when they are not working. They understand the power of leverage and are often more comfortable with taking risks.

4. I—Investor: *RIGHT SIDE OF QUADRANT*

- **Characteristics:** Investors make money by putting their money to work for them. They invest in assets like dividend-paying stocks, real estate, managed funds, or businesses that generate passive income. *Their money earns money,* creating financial freedom.
- **Mindset:** Investors prioritize financial education and understand how to assess and manage risk. They aim to achieve financial independence by having their passive income exceed their expenses.

Moving from the Left Side to the Right Side:

1. Why Shift at All?
   - Financial freedom is most achievable on the **right side** of the quadrant (**B**usiness Owner and **I**nvestor).
   - While the left side (**E**mployee and **S**elf-Employed) can provide income, it requires ongoing work and time commitment.
   - The right side offers opportunities for passive income and greater wealth creation.
2. Mindset Shift
   - Transitioning from the left side to the right side requires a significant mindset shift.
   - Employees and self-employed individuals often focus on job security and immediate earnings, while business owners and investors prioritize long-term wealth, leverage, and financial education.
3. Financial Education
   - Financial education is critical for those who want to move to the right side of the quadrant.
   - Understanding how money works, how to build and manage businesses, and how to invest wisely are crucial skills for achieving financial independence.
   - For example, just by reading this book, you're increasing your financial education. *Good for you!*

4. **The Importance of Systems**

    - ☆ For business owners, creating systems that run independently of their direct involvement is key.
    - ☆ Owning a business means owning a system and having others run that system, allowing the business owner to focus on growth and other opportunities.

5. **Passive Income and Financial Freedom**

    - ☆ The ultimate goal is to become an Investor, where your money works for you rather than you working for money.
    - ☆ Passive income—money earned without active involvement—is the path to financial freedom.

6. **Overcoming Fear and Comfort**

    - ☆ Moving to the right side of the quadrant often involves overcoming the fear of financial risk and stepping out of one's comfort zone.
    - ☆ So, take calculated risks, invest in financial education, and develop the courage to pursue opportunities that can lead to financial independence.

Quadrant Shift

Without outright admitting I'm "quadrant biased," I will let you know ... it's so much better on the right side!

Call me a "quadrantist" if you want; I won't deny it. But the benefits over on the right are massive. "Righters" enjoy

a. Favorable tax treatment
b. Financial independence
c. Leverage
d. Control
e. Scalability
f. Flexibility
g. The ability to build a lasting legacy

Those on the right get out of the "rat race" and build generational wealth. These benefits make the **B**usiness Owner and **I**nvestor quadrants superior for anyone interested in achieving long-term wealth and financial freedom. To accomplish this, investors must align with the Financial Freedom = PI > ME formulaic philosophy of creating financial security through asset-acquisition and passive investment strategies. Moving from the left to the right side of the quadrant is *not* as difficult as you may think!

Although I am a Business owner myself (having made the bulk of my income in that quadrant), I do **NOT** *recommend that route for others just getting started!*

Unless you have a business idea brewing in your head waiting to be unleashed upon the world, I would actually recommend that the most expedient path is going from the **E** to the **I** quadrant. Why? Because the quadrants are not mutually exclusive; you can straddle one foot in both quadrants at the same time and work your way over gradually!

For example, try this very practical path forward:

- ☆ Continue to work your 9–5 job as an ***E***.
- ☆ In your off hours and weekends, seek out passive investment opportunities (start feeling out the options that exists as an ***I***).
  - Personally speaking, the easiest passive income opportunities I've found are via *purchasing multi-family rental properties.*
- ☆ Squirrel money away into your **IBC Banking System** day-by-day, week-by-week (see Chapter 5: Build Your Infinite Banking System).
- ☆ **Cease all stock purchases**, 401(k) matches, and qualified plan "vesting." DIVEST from them. Take the 10% penalty and tax hit; don't worry about that employee match–*it just ain't worth what you're missing out on!*
- ☆ Reduce your discretionary spending and live as frugally as possible while you stock up on cash (see Chapters 3 and 4).

Before long you'll have amassed a sizable amount of Cash Value (CV) in your policy(ies). Leverage this to take out a policy loan for a down-payment on a multi-family property. It could be a 1bd/2ba or a 2bd/2ba to begin your journey. Starting small can produce big results! More importantly, it'll be a colossal step forward and give you confidence.

Once you have purchased your investment property, suck out that cash flow. Hire a management company and use the rental income to pay back your policy loan (play "Honest Banker"). This may take months or even years. But once you do this, **rinse and repeat!** Keep buying multi-family units that produce positive cash flow, and track your progress as you go.

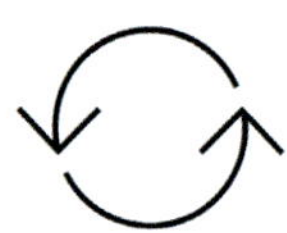

Before too long, you'll have amassed enough cash flow-producing assets to offset a significant amount of your monthly expenses. The system works. You'll be moving, slowly but surely, from the Left to the Right side of the **Cash Flow Quadrant!**

WANT A TRIAL RUN?

Wouldn't it be nice to test these concepts out in a safe environment?

Try your hand escaping the "rat race" in a risk-free environment. I highly recommend purchasing the board game *Cash flow.*

It's 10x more fun than *Monopoly* and will actively teach you (and your entire family) the principles described in this chapter in a "hands-on" way!

Summary and Takeaways

The Cash Flow Quadrant serves as a powerful roadmap for individuals looking to transition from traditional income models (i.e., your W2 job) that rely on active work (like being an employee or self-employed) to those that generate passive income (like being a **B**usiness owner or **I**nvestor).

The way you can avoid trading time for money is by escaping the "rat race" and moving from the left side to the right side of the quadrant. you do this by building up your passive income!

The takeaway is clear: by understanding which quadrant you are in and making conscious decisions to move to the Right side, you can achieve greater financial freedom and independence.

Hopefully you read this chapter as a concerted call-to-action to take control of your financial future through education, mindset shifts, and strategic, passive investments.

Taking the first few steps moving from the Left side to the Right side of the Quadrant is a decisive blow on a **Warp Whistle.** This completely changes your position in the game. It's a life-altering decision to take control of your destiny, forge your own path, and escape the Rat Race.

The path from an **E** (Employee) to an **I** (Investor) is no small undertaking! It takes years of hard work and seed capital. Finding and blowing on the other **Warp Whistles** found in this book will not only allow you to shift quadrants but get you there quicker than ever imagined.

"Most people fail to realize that in life, it's not how much money you make; it's how much money you keep!"

—Robert Kiyosaki

IRS
IBC
PLAYER 1

CHEAT CODE #8

LEGALLY AVOID TAXES

HINT

Most people think it's an expense they can't reduce or avoid.

What's the **NUMBER ONE** biggest expense nearly every person has?

... If you guessed **taxes,** you are correct!

Origin of the Income Tax

The federal income tax in the United States traces back to the early 20th century, specifically with the illegal ratification of the 16th Amendment in 1913.

Before this, due to the limits wisely imposed by the framers of the Constitution, the U.S. government relied on tariffs and excise taxes for revenue. The idea of an income tax had been introduced earlier in 1861, during the Civil War, as an extreme measure to fund the war effort but was later repealed in 1872.

When the 16th Amendment was passed, it was explicitly promoted as a temporary measure and designed to **EXCLUSIVELY tax the wealthiest Americans only**—with the solemn promise that it would NEVER affect the middle and lower classes.

Woodrow Wilson was president of the U.S. at this time and presided over two of the worst inventions in modern financial history: the creation of the income tax and the creation of the Federal Reserve.

The tax rates were initially low, starting at just 1% on income over $3,000 (equivalent to around $85,000 in today's dollars), and only rising to **6% on incomes above $500,000** (about **$14 million today**).

This framing as a **temporary, limited tax** (exclusively on the "rich") allowed it to gain public support and eased concerns about its potential impact on the broader population.

Give Them an Inch, They'll Take a Mile

By presenting the income tax as temporary and "limited in scope," lawmakers aimed to make it more politically palatable. The idea was that it would only be needed for a "short period" to address specific financial needs, such as the government's need to fund operations and to balance revenue sources as the country industrialized and wealth concentrated among the rich.

As mentioned, the tax was initially set at extremely low rates and applied **only to the wealthiest Americans,** reinforcing the notion that it was a targeted, limited measure that would not affect the broader population.

The "temporary" aspect was also linked to the political climate of the time. Politicians claimed that once the immediate financial needs were met, the income tax **could be reduced or even eliminated!** This (dishonest) marketing approach helped dupe voters by mitigating their fears of a permanent, ever-expanding tax burden.

Like clockwork, however, everything proceeded exactly as might be expected....

Akin to a camel getting its nose under the tent, once ratified the income tax quickly expanded to include a broader segment of the population and became a **permanent fixture of the U.S. tax system.**

The collective will of the American people softened. Similar to a bad magic trick, "income tax drift" began to unfold swiftly as all three lies unraveled. For the income tax turned out to be neither "temporary," "low," nor "only directed at the rich."

By 1917, just four years after the income tax was introduced, the U.S. entered World War I, which drastically increased the demand for revenue in order to fund government-sponsored mass murder campaigns (aka "war.").

To finance its mass murder campaign, Congress passed the War Revenue Act of 1917, which significantly lowered the income threshold for taxation and increased tax rates. This meant that **middle-class Americans, who were not initially subject to the tax, began to be taxed.**

By the end of World War I, about **5%** of the U.S. population was paying federal income taxes, a significant increase from the less than 1% who paid in 1913.

Over the following decades, particularly during the Great Depression and World War II, the tax base expanded even further.

The Revenue Act of 1942, passed during World War II, marked a major turning point as it lowered the income threshold even more and introduced *payroll withholding*, making income tax a required obligation for millions of Americans, including many in the working and middle classes. This also helped blind Americans to the true cost of taxation, as the taxes came right out of their paychecks!

As such, it essentially took roughly 25 to 30 years from 1913 for the introduction of a "very low" and "temporary" income tax "targeted exclusively on the rich" to become a "normal" and oppressive tax imposed on everyday Americans.

Today's Income Tax Rates

Today, everyone and their grandmother is subject to the oppressive income tax. It is technically a "progressive" income tax with different rates impacting different income levels.

Here are the current income tax brackets, as of 2025:

- **10%:** Applies to income up to $11,925 for single filers, $23,850 for married couples filing jointly, and $17,000 for heads of household.

- **12%:** Applies to income over $11,925 up to $48,475 for single filers, over $23,851 up to $96,950 for married couples filing jointly, and over $17,001 up to $64,850 for heads of household.
- **22%:** Applies to income over $48,476 up to $103,350 for single filers, over $96,951 up to 206,700 for married couples filing jointly, and over $64,851 up to $103,350 for heads of household.
- **24%:** Applies to income over $103,351 up to $197,300 for single filers, over $206,701 up to $394,600 for married couples filing jointly, and over $103,351 up to $197,300 for heads of household.
- **32%:** Applies to income over $197,301 up to $250,525 for single filers, over $394,601 up to $501,050 for married couples filing jointly, and over $197,301 up to $250,500 for heads of household.
- **35%:** Applies to income over $250,526 up to $626,350 for single filers, over $501,051 up to $751,600 for married couples filing jointly, and over $250,501 up to $626,350 for heads of household.
- **37%:** Applies to income over $626,351 for single filers, over $751,601 for married couples filing jointly, and over $626,351 for heads of household.

So, let this be a lesson to you. Whenever you hear the government is introducing a "temporary" or "emergency" spending or taxation bill, be wary.

Be extremely wary!

"For nothing is so permanent as a temporary government program."
—Milton Friedman

It took only a single generation for a supposed "temporary" tax that was ONLY supposed to be imposed on the super-duper-uber rich to quickly be used as a weapon to also bludgeon the poor and middle class.

Government propaganda, war, and the misguided perception for an increased need to expand public services codified a lie ("it's all just temporary") and shifted the immense (and growing) tax burden from the rich to the poor.

But what exactly are income taxes...?

Taxation Is Theft and a Criminal Penalty on Success

Income taxes are, quite plainly, theft. Income tax is a ruthless, criminal penalty imposed on success. When you are taxed upwards of 35–37% of your income (and that's just federal taxes), you have just had 35–37% of your productivity *robbed from you.*

For example, if you work 40 hours in a week but are only paid for 26 of those hours, the amount of money you're owed for working those extra 14 hours was simply STOLEN from you! Fourteen hours of your life was effectively robbed from you because of taxes!

Taxes are enforced by a democratically elected mafia-like organization called the U.S. government, which wields its power to extort funds from those who are productive.

Just like any criminal fine, taxes disincentivize the behavior that incurs the penalty.

For example, speeding tickets exist to disincentivize speeding; the faster you travel above the speed limit, the higher your fine (your "speeding tax"). The U.S. government also institutes harsh fines ("taxes") on cigarettes—because, accurately, the health impacts of cigarettes are believed to be a net negative to society. Thus, these taxes are meant to discourage cigarette consumption. And it works.

The U.S. government implements other "sin taxes" on products such as alcohol and gambling for similar reasons. These taxes, in theory, are meant to dissuade people from participating in these so-called "sinful" activities.

So, when the government implements a **progressive income tax** on society it is, in effect, curtailing the amount of productive work, profitability, and success of its citizens.

Taxes are a fine on both productivity and success. The more you work or the more successful you are, the higher your fine becomes.

Consider the axiom: if you want more of something, you subsidize it; if you want less of something, you tax it.

Thus, it makes little sense to implement a fine ("tax") on productivity and prosperity if the intended goal is to encourage more of it. Yet this is what happens. It is simply the framework of reality we must all operate within.

That said, one of the absolute best Warp Whistles you can find is the one that allows you to **legally lower or eliminate your taxes**—just like the rich do!

The Rich Don't Pay Taxes

The majority of the rich legally do not pay taxes.

I'll say that again. ***The rich don't pay taxes!***

Why? Cry about it all you want, but the rich do this simply because they are able to *take advantage of the existing tax code.*

Did you know that the U.S. Tax Code is 6,871 pages long? Roughly 19 pages of the tax code are devoted to describing what is owed by persons and organizations, with respect to the income tax.

The remaining ~6,852 pages exist to describe, in intricate detail, all the ways to **AVOID** those taxes through legal incentives and deductions.

Tax-Free Wealth by Tom Wheelwright

No person is better equipped to describe the tax code and map out all the ways to leverage it to decrease one's tax burden than Tom Wheelwright.

His book *Tax-Free Wealth* is a comprehensive guide to understanding and leveraging the tax code to maximize wealth and minimize taxes legally. The book is part of Robert Kiyosaki's Rich Dad series (Tom is Robert's CPA).

In the book, Wheelwright offers strategies that help individuals and business owners leverage the **Cash Flow Quadrant** (see Chapter 7: Move to the Right Side of the Quadrant) and take full advantage of the tax benefits available to them. Below is a very brief summary of the most efficient tax benefits and tax-saving strategies highlighted in the book:

1. Understanding the Tax Code as a Roadmap

- ☆ **The Tax Code's Purpose:** Wheelwright emphasizes that the tax code is not just a set of rules to collect taxes but a series of incentives that governments use to encourage certain behaviors. Understanding this perspective allows individuals and businesses to align their activities with these incentives and reduce their tax liabilities.
- ☆ **Strategy:** Approach the tax code as a roadmap for financial planning. The more you align your financial activities with government incentives (such as investing in real estate, starting businesses, or participating in energy conservation), the more tax benefits you can unlock.

2. Real Estate Investment for Depreciation and Deductions

- ☆ **Depreciation:** One of the most significant tax benefits in real estate is the ability to depreciate property. Depreciation allows you to deduct a portion of the cost of a property each year, reducing taxable income without impacting cash flow.
- ☆ **Bonus Depreciation:** Recent tax laws allow for 100% bonus depreciation, where you can accelerate depreciation on certain types of property improvements, leading to larger deductions in the early years of ownership.
  - This feeds extremely well into the **PI > ME** strategy of buying cash flow-producing assets. Because now you can have your cake and eat it too! You can purchase an asset that throws off passive income AND for many years also take advantage of that income completely **tax-free** using the bonus depreciation as a legal write-off ("loss in the first year").

- ☆ **Strategy:** Invest in real estate and take full advantage of depreciation to reduce taxable income. Leverage cost segregation studies to break down property into various components, which can then be depreciated at different rates, increasing the potential deductions.

3. Business Ownership and Deductible Expenses

- ☆ **Business Deductions:** Owning a business provides numerous opportunities for tax deductions. Common deductible expenses include operating costs, salaries, equipment, office supplies, and even a home office if part of your residence is primarily used for business purposes.
- ☆ **The Importance of Structuring:** Wheelwright emphasizes the importance of proper business structuring. By choosing the right legal structure (e.g., LLC, S-Corp), you can optimize tax benefits. For instance, an S-Corp allows business owners to split income between salary and distributions, potentially reducing self-employment taxes (more on this below).
- ☆ **Strategy:** Start or buy a business to take advantage of the wide range of deductible expenses. Ensure your business is structured correctly to maximize tax savings.

4. Leveraging Tax Credits

- ☆ **Tax Credits vs. Deductions:** Unlike deductions, which reduce taxable income, tax credits reduce the amount of tax owed directly, making them more valuable. There are various credits, such as the Research and Development (R&D) tax credit, which is available to businesses that innovate or improve products.
- ☆ **Energy Efficiency Credits:** There are also credits available for investing in renewable energy or making energy-efficient improvements to your home or business.
- ☆ **Strategy:** Identify and claim all available tax credits relevant to your personal and business activities. For businesses, particularly look into R&D credits and energy efficiency incentives.

5. Using Tax-Free Exchanges (Like-Kind Exchanges)

- ☆ **1031 Exchange:** The 1031 Exchange allows real estate investors to defer capital gains taxes when they sell a property, as long as the proceeds are reinvested in a similar type of property within 180 days. This strategy enables investors to continue building wealth without paying taxes on gains immediately.
- ☆ **Strategy:** If you own investment properties, use a 1031 Exchange to defer capital gains taxes and keep more capital working for you.

6. Health Savings Accounts (HSAs)

- ☆ **Triple Tax Advantage:** HSAs provide a triple tax benefit: contributions are tax-deductible, the funds grow tax-free, and withdrawals for qualified medical expenses are tax-free. This makes HSAs one of the most tax-efficient ways to save for healthcare costs.
- ☆ **Strategy:** Maximize contributions to an HSA if you are eligible, particularly if you have a high-deductible health plan. Use the funds for qualified medical expenses or let them grow for future use.

7. Tax Loss Harvesting

- ☆ **Offsetting Gains:** Tax loss harvesting involves selling investments at a loss to offset capital gains from other investments. This strategy can reduce the amount of capital gains taxes owed.
- ☆ **Strategy:** Regularly review your investment portfolio to identify opportunities for tax loss harvesting, especially at year-end. This can significantly reduce your overall tax liability on investment income.

8. Charitable Contributions

- ☆ **Deductible Donations:** Charitable contributions are deductible if you itemize your deductions. Donating appreciated assets, like stocks, rather than cash, can be particularly advantageous because you can avoid capital gains taxes on the appreciation.

- ☆ **Donor-Advised Funds:** Consider setting up a donor-advised fund, which allows you to make a large deductible donation in one year and distribute the funds to charities over time.
- ☆ **Strategy:** Make charitable contributions strategically, focusing on appreciated assets and leveraging donor-advised funds to maximize deductions.

9. Estate Planning and Wealth Transfer

- ☆ **Estate Tax Strategies:** There are various strategies for minimizing estate taxes, including gifting strategies, setting up revocable trusts, and making use of the lifetime gift tax exemption.
- ☆ **Step-Up in Basis:** One powerful tax benefit in estate planning is the step-up in basis, where inherited assets receive a new tax basis equal to their market value at the time of the owner's death. This can significantly reduce capital gains taxes for heirs.
- ☆ **Strategy:** Meet with and estate planner and develop a comprehensive estate plan that includes gifting, trusts, and the use of the step-up in basis to minimize taxes on wealth transfer.

10. Tax Planning and Professional Advice

- ☆ **Proactive Tax Planning:** One cannot emphasize enough the importance of proactive tax planning. Waiting until the end of the year or after filing taxes is too late to take advantage of many tax-saving opportunities.
- ☆ **Using Tax Professionals:** I strongly recommend you work with a seasoned tax professional who understands the tax code and can help you implement these strategies effectively.
- ☆ **Strategy:** Engage in proactive tax planning throughout the year and work closely with a knowledgeable tax advisor to ensure you are maximizing your tax benefits.

11. Combine Multiple Business Entities for Tax Purposes

☆ **S-Corps Avoid Self-Employment Taxes:** Wheelwright explains near the end of the book the benefits of using the appropriate business entity to minimize unnecessary taxes.

For example, he explains the benefits of the S-Corp entity and the fact its structure does not have to pay the self-employment taxes like an LLC does.

☆ **Strategy**:

- Work with a CPA and set up an S-Corporation.
- Transfer the ownership of assets so that the S-Corp now owns any/all LLCs—vs. you owning these LLCs individually.
- Have the S-Corp pay you a W2 salary (a salary that's set based on your legitimate hours in the business that is fair and legally derived).
- From the W2 salary will be where all FICA taxes are paid and will represent the 7.65% (employer) + 7.65% (employee) totaling to the 15.3% total tax owed. **This tax is paid only on the W2 salary portion of your income.**
- The remaining income from the business will be paid to you in the form of dividends/distributions.
- This simple and creative solution can legally avoid many tens of thousands of unnecessary self-employment taxes by splitting off the FICA taxes into just the smaller "W2" component of your income.

12. Paying Your Children an Income

☆ **Strategy:** You can pay your children a reasonable salary for working in your business, up to a certain amount each year. For 2025, this amount is up to **$15,000 per child** (the limit may change each year). Since this amount is under the standard deduction for individuals, it's generally tax-free for the child. Meanwhile, the business owner can deduct this salary as a business expense, reducing taxable income.

- ☆ **Application:** This strategy is effective when children perform legitimate work for the business. Examples could include filing, managing social media, or other appropriate tasks. This also teaches children about work and money management while benefiting from tax savings.

13. Renting Your Home for Business Meetings

- ☆ **Strategy:** The tax code allows homeowners to rent out their home for up to 14 days per year without having to report the rental income. Business owners can take advantage of this by renting their home to their business for meetings or events. The business can deduct the rental expense as a business cost, but the homeowner (who is also the business owner) *does not have to report the rental income* if it's for 14 days or fewer per year.
- ☆ **Application:** Ensure that the rental arrangement is legitimate, with fair market value rent, and document the purpose of the meetings or events. This can be a tax-efficient way to take money out of the business tax-free.

14. Become a Real Estate Professional

- ☆ **Strategy:** The tax code allows individuals who spend 50% of their workweek (750 hours or more per year) on real estate activities to be classified as *real estate professionals*. Activities like property management, leasing, real estate development, or buying/selling properties apply. In general, any work related to real estate investing will count! Once you OR YOUR SPOUSE become a real estate professional, you can take advantage of the massive tax benefit of writing off depreciation against your ***active*** income!
- ☆ **Application:** Depreciation (which Tom Wheelwright calls the "magic deduction") typically can be written off against one's *passive* income only. However, if you (or your spouse) become real estate professionals, it unlocks a huge Warp Whistle! For example, this can be a game-changer if one spouse works a 9–5 W2 job and the other spouse is a homemaker. Getting certified as a *real estate professional* would allow ALL your real estate deprecation to be used to as a write off against the family's W2 (***active***) income! That's HUGE!

Parting Shots at Government Thieves

The rich don't pay taxes because they take the time to understand the massive advantages of a salient tax strategy (or at least their CPAs do).

If you are not paying attention to your taxes, you are basically allowing 30–50%+ of your money to be extorted from you without a fight!

FIGHT. FIGHT. FIGHT!

Please. Don't give up without a fight.

Oppression, extortion, and theft sadly are very real and cruel parts of this life. A vile and duplicitous organization calling themselves the U.S. government will inevitably use "legal plunder" to steal and arrest YOUR money.

For as Benjamin Franklin once said, "In this world, nothing is certain except death and taxes."

However, a simple *Warp Whistle* will allow Franklin to eat his words!

"I would like to electrocute everyone who uses the word 'fair' in connection with income tax policies."
—William F. Buckley, Jr.

Luckily there are legal ways to avoid or defer having your property stolen from you. Keep more in your pocket and use it to give to those in need, help family and friends, and invest more in your future.

The more wealth you have stolen from you, the less you have for yourself and those you care about; the less you are able to tithe or give the charity; and the less you are able to invest in assets and create generational wealth.

This chapter was just a very brief primer on a complex and nuanced topic. I strongly encourage you to read *Tax-Free Wealth* by Tom Wheelwright. Its pages provide a far more detailed and comprehensive roadmap for legally reducing taxes and maximizing wealth than found here.

By understanding and applying the tax code strategically, individuals and business owners can significantly reduce their tax liabilities, avoid as much "legal plunder" as possible, and increase their financial success. I personally find that the two (2) most pragmatic components related to efficient and prudent tax strategy are:

1. **Real estate investments** due to the use of *depreciation* as a "miracle" tax writeoff.
2. **Business ownership** and all its *many* beneficial tax deductions and writeoffs.

DID YOU KNOW?
Businesses pay all their **expenses** *before* paying taxes. However, employees pay their **taxes** *before* paying expenses!

Taxes are a business's (or person's) *largest and most significant expense*; however, with knowledge and a solid strategy, a sound investor can blow into a **Warp Whistle** and cut some, most, or perhaps even ALL of their tax burden—which, in turn, allows them to keep more of their own property and build lasting wealth for their family.

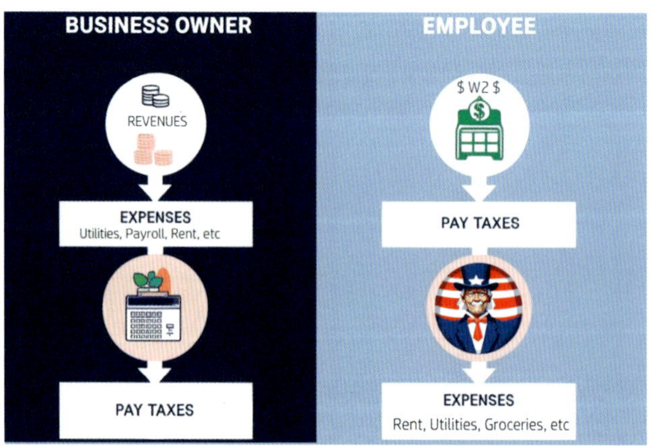

"Taxation is theft, purely and simply even though it is theft on a grand and colossal scale which no acknowledged criminals could hope to match."

—Murray N. Rothbard

PI > ME
PI < ME
HIGH SCORE!
PLAYER 1

CHEAT CODE #9

GAMIFY YOUR INVESTING

Probably one of the easiest and most practical steps anyone can take after reading this book is to GAMIFY their investing strategy.

I've already written about blowing into Warp Whistles and magically catapulting from World 1 ('Normal' W2 income / Left Side of the Cash Flow Quadrant) to World 9 (Building Passive Income Streams / PI > ME). So why not take it a step further, and make the entire process a game?

By this, I don't just mean something generic like "have fun." Stupid advice like that should make you vomit in your mouth a little bit.

I mean quite literally—make investing a game and the PI > ME tracking process part your regular routine.

Here's what I mean. If you've been paying attention, there were several investing concepts that almost every author referenced in this book has highlighted as being super important. One of them was **budgeting.**

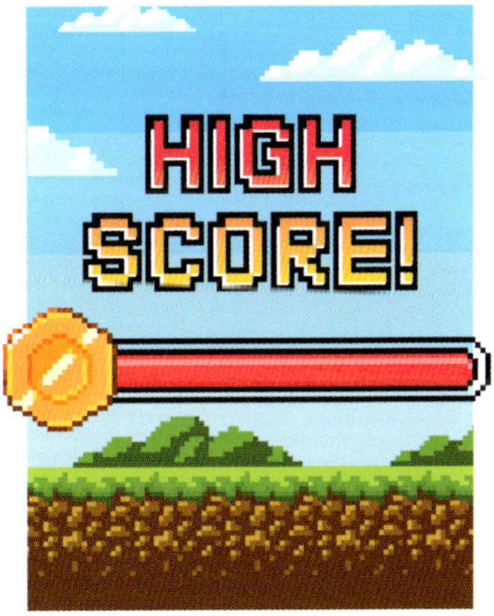

In order to track how well you're doing in any game, you must keep score!

Your BUDGET is one half of your **PI > ME** scorecard. It tracks the Monthly Expenses side of the equation
Financial Freedom = PI > ME.

I'm going to ingrain this formula into your head before you finish this book.

It needs to be what you think about during the day and what you think about when you go to bed at night; it should be what you dream about and what wakes you up in the morning. Here it is again, nice and big and beautiful.

Financial Freedom =

A wise man once said, "What you track grows; what you track and report on grows exponentially."

BUDGET, BUDGET, BUDGET!

Monthly Expense Budgeting

You must **budget** and track your expenses. From Clason to Ramsey to Kiyosaki and Wheelwright—they all scream the same thing.

If you don't budget and track your expenses, you're flying blind. Ramsey calls the budgeting process "giving every dollar a name" (see Chapter 3).

Figure out EXACTLY where your money is going. Be brutally honest with yourself. And don't just guess! Pull open your *Quickbooks* account or your *Quicken* account or your *Monarch Money* account.

If you don't have one of these apps set up yet, **START TODAY**. But before doing so, download the last 12–24 months' worth of bank statements. Go through them with a fine-tooth comb and line-by-line. Write it all down.

Where is your money going? Don't guess. *Find out!* Give each dollar a name!

I recommend tracking your monthly expenses into three (3) high-level buckets:

- ☆ **Fixed Expenses** (e.g., subscriptions and monthly payments that don't change in their amount. They're fixed payments.)
  - Your Netflix subscription, car payment, or mortgage payment fit into this bucket.
- ☆ **Variable Expenses** (e.g., monthly payments that are required to live but the amounts vary from month to month).
  - Your utility bills, vehicle fuel cost, and grocery bills fit into this bucket.
- ☆ **Discretionary Expenses** (e.g., items that you don't precisely NEED but know you'll be spending money on. And don't fool yourself—you gotta splurge now and then)
  - Starbucks coffee, restaurants (eating out), vacations, and your golf outings all fit into this bucket.

I highly recommend putting your formal budget into some form of software. You can use plain ol' Microsoft Excel, which gives you complete flexibility over the layout and presentation of the data. Creating spreadsheets in MS Excel is a skill everyone should master.

For my personal budgeting, I prefer to use an online tool like Monarch Money (ever since Mint shut down). However, I hear that EveryDollar also is a great tool. For my business budgeting, I use Quickbooks. Whatever you use, get your numbers in place and then track them *diligently*.

When I say diligently, I mean it. Make it a game! Gamify your budgeting process. And take the game seriously.

See if you can come in at or under your budget each month for every category. If you set a $800/mo budget for your groceries, stick to that budget! If you *must* cheat (e.g., you're nearing the end of the month and you've spent $794 on groceries and the only thing left in the fridge is ketchup), then you know your budget either isn't calibrated right (you weren't accurate when looking at past data) OR you had some rare "one-off" purchases (anomalies) skew the results.

If you encounter these situations, don't fret. But honor the rules of the game. You'll have to "steal" from another budget line item to pay for your groceries. Rob untapped funds from your restaurant budget so you can now get groceries. And yes, this may mean you won't be able to go out to eat that month since you were a poor planner and didn't properly budget. Boo hoo!

This isn't an exercise in sadism; it's meant to ensure you are being honest with yourself by honoring your budget. You must respect the game! Because if your budget has no teeth, it's not doing you any good.

Track your progress *at least* monthly. Ideally weekly. Are your numbers accurate? Are they staying on track? Are they under? Over? Be honest.

Any extra money you wind up with at the end of the month goes where...? Yep, right into your **Infinite Banking System** (see Chapter 5)!

Track Your Passive Income Streams

I'll be honest: as much fun as tracking your budget can be, when you begin to actively track your PASSIVE INCOME, that's always a LOT more exciting. It's a far more enjoyable game!

There's something about tracking income that is just inherently more rewarding than tracking your expenses. Maybe that's just me. But just as diligently as you track your monthly expenses, track your monthly passive income.

Just like your budget, your passive income may come in multiple forms. I suggest tracking it by category (asset class) and tier. Passive income sources often have variable amounts which change or are paid at irregular periods (e.g., quarterly instead of monthly). So, when this is the case, break everything down to average monthly passive income so you have an apples-to-apples comparison for your PI > ME calculation.

A potential categorization of passive income might look like this:

- Real Estate (Multi-family)—broken out by property address
- Managed Fund income
- Personal Loan income
- Affiliate Marketing income
- Web or Mobile App income
- Business Dividends or Guaranteed Payments
- Bond Coupon payments
- Royalties
- Recurring Sales Commissions
- Crypto mining income *(mind you, this is the ONLY form of passive income from crypto)*

I don't choose to put stock dividends on this list as they're better to put in a *DRIP* (***D**ividend **R**e-**I**nvestment **P**rogram*) vs. taking the dividends directly.

Break down each passive investment you have as its own line item. And then, based on historical average(s) or fixed payment of the asset, track its monthly income.

Now Compare the Two!

Remember the formula?

Financial Freedom –

You now have a list of your monthly Passive Income (PI) streams.

You also have your Monthly Expenses budget (ME).

Compare them! The results might look something like this:

Monthly Expense	Category	Monthly Cost	Annual Cost
Mortgage Payment	Fixed	$3,500.00	$42,000.00
Car Loan Payment	Fixed	$575.00	$6,900.00
Cellphone Bill	Fixed	$62.00	$744.00
Charity (10% Tithe)	Variable	$1,000.00	$12,000.00
Groceries	Variable	$950.00	$11,400.00
Gas/Fuel	Variable	$150.00	$1,800.00
Netflix Subscription	Fixed	$15.49	$185.88
Hulu Subscription	Fixed	$7.99	$95.88
	TOTAL:	**$6,260.48**	

Passive Income Stream	Category	Monthly Cash flow	Annual Income
305 Cedar St (4-unit) *[Tier 2]*	Multi-family	$2,100.00	$25,200.00
2 Alex Court (4bd) *[Tier 3]*	STR	$1,250.00	$15,000.00
122 Washington Ave (3-unit) *[Tier 2]*	Multi-family	$1,622.00	$19,464.00
Oil and Gas Fund *[Tier 4]*	Managed Fund	$520.00	$6,240.00
5YR Loan to Sister *[Tier 2]*	Private Lending	$950.00	$11,400.00
	TOTAL:	**$6,442.00**	

Well, check that out! If my math skills are accurate, PI > ME, because:

$6,442.00 > $6,260.48

When Passive Income exceeds Monthly Expenses, financial freedom is achieved! You win the game! This lucky investor shown above could, in theory, exit the rat race tomorrow and quit his/her job if they wanted.

That said, if you look closely, you'll see that one of these passive investments is a short-term 5YR note. So, it might be on the safe side to buy just one or two additional cash flow-producing assets first, as that passive loan income will eventually dry up.

Don't Let the Game End!

By gamifying the budgeting processing as well as the process of building passive, cash flow-producing assets (and tracking them closely), you'll be well-positioned for long-term success!

"That which is measured improves. That which is measured and reported improves exponentially!"

—Karl Pearson

Once you start, don't stop. Creating new passive income streams is contagious. The Warp Whistles that brought you here are addicting to use. Keep practicing and rehearsing with them!

Keep budgeting and tracking every dollar you spend. And keep comparing your **P**assive **I**ncome against your **M**onthly **E**xpenses. It's the most lucrative game you'll ever play!

"A budget is people telling their money where to go instead of wondering where it went."

—John Maxwell

+XP!
PLAYER 1

CHEAT CODE #10

LEARN TO IDENTIFY GREAT DEALS

This may sound odd, but the biggest obstacle holding back your success ... is you. Passive income opportunities are out there waiting to be found and acted upon.

If you fail to even look—or if you spot a deal but *refuse to act*, you're your own worst enemy.

Many things can stop a deal in its tracks. **Analysis paralysis** is the most common hurdle, especially with "newbies" to passive investing. Over-analyzing an investment opportunity often leads to one of two negative outcomes, summed up by these simple statements:

1. "It sounds too good to be true; I'm skeptical. I'll pass."
2. "I don't know what I'm doing yet; I'll hold off."

The first negative outcome is one caused by skepticism, fear, and doubt. These are human emotions. It is also a byproduct of a **scarcity mindset.** You have only a fixed amount of money to invest, and you naturally don't want to lose what little you have.

The second negative outcome is caused by a lack of financial literacy. As Kiyosaki explains in his books, this can be easily overcome with learning, training, and mentorship by others with experience.

Pro Tip: *Joining (or forming)* ***a group of other investors*** *is the #1 best way to overcome both challenges!*

Learn to Spot a Good Deal When You See One!

Analyzing a good deal isn't as complex as one might think. At a high level, a good deal will exhibit the following characteristics:

- ☆ It will be **passive** for the investor (this is a firm requirement).
- ☆ It will allow the investor to get 100% of their invested capital back within 3-6 years (via any number of means, including **refinancing, rental income payments, distributions, asset sale,** etc.)
- ☆ It will make efficient use of leverage (i.e., "paying 100% cash" for an asset is a very poor way to invest—don't do it!)
- ☆ You will be able to exert **control** over the purchased asset (see Chapter 1).
- ☆ The asset will be **collateralizable** (see Chapter 1).
- ☆ There will be **cash flow flexibility** as well as exit strategies related to the asset. For example, if it's a rental property, you'll have multiple ways to modify cash flow, such as increasing the rents, lowering the operating costs, improving the building, leveraging the asset's equity, or exiting the investment entirely via a sale.
- ☆ It'll have good financial metrics:
    - For example, a real estate investor wants to examine the **Cash-on-Cash Return (COC),** the **Return on Investment (ROI),** or the **Return on Equity (ROE).**
    - The ROI must significantly beat the opportunity cost of capital (i.e., the the rate of return for the next best *alternative* investment). Ideally the investment should beat the "risk-free" rate (e.g., a government bond) by 5-10X+ (or more).
- ☆ A **pro forma** should be presented. The pro forma should be honest, as accurate as possible, vetted, and clearly demonstrate a reasonable and consistent cash flow.
- ☆ The operator will have a long and successful **track record.**

A good deal should exhibit most, ideally ALL, of the above characteristics. If it fails to perform at any of these levels, be wary. Otherwise, **dive in!**

The fun and encouraging thing about finding deals is that it is far better to hit three or four "singles" than wait by the sidelines for an elusive "grand slam" (aka that "once in a lifetime deal").

Grand slams will come. But they'll come when you least suspect them. And they'll usually come AFTER a "single" is already guaranteed. For example, you may find something out about an opportunity after your investment is already made—which turns that single into a double, triple, or home run after the fact!

Finding the hidden Warp Whistle is learning how to identify and vet good deals. Blowing into your Warp Whistle is showing courage and TAKING ACTION—crossing the Rubicon and investing in the passive income opportunities that you uncover. Don't sit on the sidelines and over-analyze! Not every deal will be a homerun; just accept that and know it's far better to regularly and consistently hit singles and doubles.

NB: Just like "chasing yield" is a poor man's folly (see Chapter 5), so too is failing to act and holding out for that the elusive "once in a lifetime deal."

You won't escape the rat race by standing in the corner holding onto your cash watching deals go by.

When investing in passive assets, you'll achieve success just like the turtle from the story "The Tortoise and the Hare."

He reached the finish line one slow step at a time and by having the patience and diligence required to finish the race.

The hares always run out of steam midway through the race or get diverted off track by something which obfuscates or confuses their dream of winning.

For example, they chase after yield; they tilt at windmills. They are hopelessly distracted by some shiny new coin they see on the side of the road. However, the tortoise holds to the path, putting one foot after the other. The tortoise wins the race due to grit and perseverance.

Homeruns Do Exist

That all said, there are times in life when prime market conditions or extraordinary operators create opportunities that you may never see again. When this happens, *don't look a gift-horse in the mouth.*

This is happening right now. Professional investors and local business operators all over the country are actively finding "the diamonds in the rough" every single day.

For example, real estate professional Timothy Baxter from New Hampshire is one such investor making incredible deals happen for passive investors in a way that, on paper, seems almost too good to be true.

Ergo, whenever the pro forma numbers pencil-out, the operator's record is flawless, and the business plan has been vetted and shown to work—the best thing one can do is carpe diem—"seize the day"!

In Baxter's case, he is leveraging extensive networks to find multi-family rental deals off market with the per-unit price below typical retail prices. Moreso, he guarantees investors their **entire principal** of invested capital back within **24 months or less** via a refinance and post-stabilization of rents. That is about 2 (almost 3) times faster than typical real estate deals!

Baxter also assumes 100% of the risk, taking on any/all capital calls required by new property purchases (e.g., if a new roof is needed, he funds the Capital Expenditure ("CAPEX"), not the investors). Lastly, Baxter offers investors the tremendous tax benefits of **accelerated depreciation,** making the first several years of cash flow **completely tax-free!**

A deal like this checks all the boxes!

So, investment grand-slams do, in fact, exist. And when they are offered, **grab at them with both hands!** Unique opportunities don't last forever.

The Investment Cycle (aka "Deal Flow")

Okay, this part is important. You need to keep your Investment Cycle moving. Get proactive and engaged. Get into the groove! Your money should always be moving....

If your money isn't working for you, it's working against you.

A stagnant pool of capital is not proactive. Funds sitting idle, like unpicked grapes, often die on the vine. Don't forget about inflation!

If your capital is sitting unused for too long, it's slowly losing purchasing power. Your IBC Bank is a critical defense against inflation, but it's not 100% insulating you. Your IBC Bank is simply PRESERVING your capital; it's not growing it (when adjusting for inflation)!

You must invest in cash flow-producing assets to avoid the government's pernicious "inflation tax."

As such, your cycle of funding and investing in new deals should ideally look like this as a constantly moving CIRCLE of steps:

☆ **SEED CAPITAL**—Fund your IBC policy(ies) (see Chapter 5).

- Build up a reservoir of Tier 1 capital in your "bank" which you'll ultimately use to invest!
- NB: Initially you may need to allow 4–7 years for the capital to grow enough to fund your first few deals.
- Windfalls can greatly expedite the process! (e.g., the sale of an asset, an inheritance, etc.)

☆ **RESEARCH**—Explore investment opportunities.

- Bone-up on your financial literacy!

- Examine the financial metrics of prospective deals.
- As mentioned previously, this could be starting a new business or opening a franchise. Or perhaps making private loans to friends or colleagues.
- But I personally prefer to invest in juicy, sexy, faithful REAL ESTATE deals! It's the easiest way to move from an E (or S) to an I (see Chapter 7).

☆ **ACTION**—Buy the investment!

- Take out a policy loan from your IBC Bank for the down payment on the investment (20–25% down).
- Note: you are still going to use LEVERAGE (i.e., a commercial mortgage) to fund the remaining 80–85%.

☆ **CASH FLOW**—Suck up the net income ("cash flow") from the asset.

☆ **REINVEST**—Use the cash flow to provide Seed Capital!

- Use the cash flow from the asset to pay down your policy loan.
- Once the loan is paid off, reinvest that cash flow back into your policy as either Paid-Up Additions (aka "Lump Sums") OR if the policy is "maxed out" then open up a NEW policy to expand your IBC Banking System (see Chapter 5).

Graphically, the **Investment Cycle** looks like this:

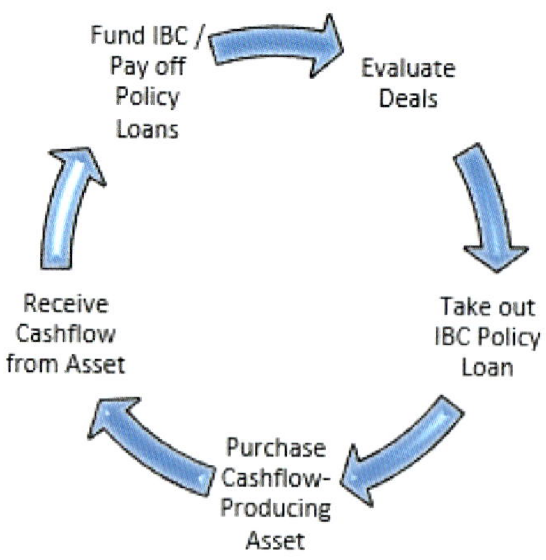

Your **deal flow** is important; it keeps your money moving (you want your money making you money, remember?) and it moves you in the direction of creating cash flow-producing assets so you can exit the 'rat race.'

The velocity of money going through your *banking system* and **Investment Cycle** is critical to your success! The knowledge, opportunity, capital, and gumption required to employ the Cycle depicted above is a super valuable **Warp Whistle!** Pick it up. Use it!

What opportunities may surface as the economy dips into a recession or inflation continues to soar? Only time will tell....

But I will tell you one thing—**keep your IBC Bank well fed** so you have plenty of dry powder for coming deals on the investment horizon!

And don't forget to bone-up on your financial literacy along the way! Learn how to read critical financial statements, such as **Profit and Loss Statements, Balance Sheets, pro formas, rent rolls, ROI analysis**, and **NPV calculations** so that you can properly differentiate a bad deal from a good deal, and a good deal from a great one.

Once you can do that, you've located yet another Warp Whistle that will send you even deeper into the world of lucrative investing.

Rinse and Repeat! A Real Estate Example

Let's put everything together with a single example. At the risk of being repetitive, here again is the Investment Cycle and associated concepts required to invest in a cash flow-producing real estate asset:

- ☆ Save up funds for 4–7 years by "Paying Yourself First" (see Chapter 4) and deposit every dime you can into your IBC Policy (see Chapter 5). This capitalizes your Bank!
- ☆ Find a real estate deal that allows you to cash flow ~$1,000–$1,500+/mo.
    - E.g., after some research you locate a "base hit": a $315,000 3-unit multi-family property with a property management company already in place to manage it.

- It has three units; each unit is a 2bd/2ba in an area that will support $1,600/mo for rent. ($1,600 x 3 = $4,800/mo revenue)
- The mortgage will be $1,511/mo. Other expenses related to the property will be $1,800/mo. Total expenses = $3,311/mo
- So, after paying all expenses as well as the mortgage, you net $1,489/mo profit (this is your "Cash flow").
- This investment requires a $75K down payment to purchase (20% of purchase price plus closing costs)

☆ Take out a policy loan for the $75K using your **IBC Bank.**

☆ Hire a firm to do a **Cost Segregation Study** on the property. Depreciate as much as you can in year 1 using bonus depreciation. (See Chapter 8.)

- This allows you to take a massive paper "loss" due to DEPRECIATION expense of the building. All the rental income it generates for the next several years will be TAX FREE!

☆ Suck the cash flow out of the deal and use the $1,489/mo (tax-free!) income to slowly pay off the $75K policy loan ("Play Honest Banker," see Chapter 4). In just over four years, you'll pay the policy loan back in full, replenishing your CV so you can make more deals!

☆ Do it again!!!!!

- That worked pretty well, didn't it? Do it again. Buy another one!
- By this time, you will likely have enough Tier 1 capital in your IBC Bank to purchase a 4-, 5- or even 6-unit rental property!

☆ Keep following this process!! ***Rinse and repeat.***

☆ As you move forward, you will slowly build various "cash flow silos" of passive income—each one flowing back into and through your banking system.

- Each Silo flows FROM your Bank (investment capital) as well as back TOWARDS your Bank (cash flow).

☆ Each Silo also does two things:

- It creates an asset (and associated liability) on your Balance Sheet.
- It creates consistent CASH FLOW for you (i.e., passive income) on your income Statement!

- ☆ TRACK YOUR PROGRESS: You now have ~$1,500/mo in your Passive Income section of your spreadsheet to track in your PI > ME Reporting (See Chapter 9).
  - Track your PI > ME after each deal as you expand.

When your PI > ME, quit your job! You've used your Warp Whistles all together and beaten the game! You are now financially free! Congratulations!

Graphically, the results may look like this after your deal flow gets going:

YOUR IBC BANKING SYSTEM:

3-unit MF	4-unit MF	4-unit MF	4-unit MF	6-unit MF
$1,489/mo	$2,000/mo	$2,100/mo	$2,000/mo	$3,100/mo

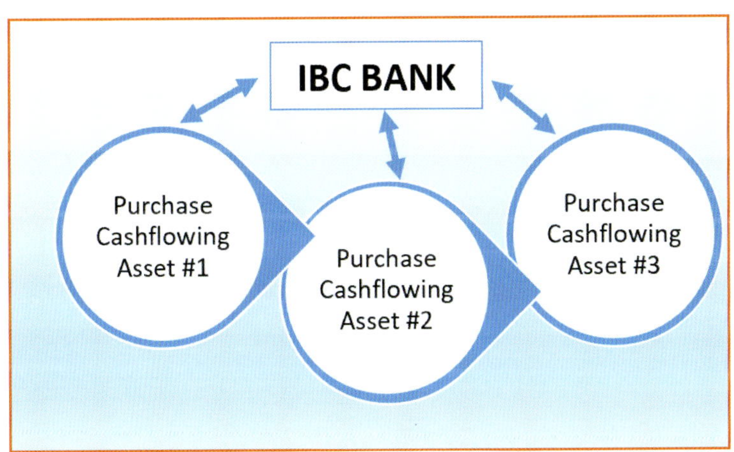

Each "Silo" of your passive income is pulling passive income into your bank (as well as feeding from your bank for the initial investment funds).

When you sum up all the passive cash flows ($10,689/mo in the above example) you COMPARE that number with your Monthly Expenses. Which number is greater?

When your Passive Income (PI) is greater than your Monthly Expenses (ME), *drop the mic*. That **Warp Whistle** sure makes beautiful music!

COLLEGE DIPLOMA
PLAYER 1

CHEAT CODE #11

AVOID THE COLLEGE TRAP

If you have already graduated from college and have no children nearing college age, feel free to skip this chapter. Otherwise, please continue, my dear faithful reader. This pertains to you....

Cost and Mission Drift

The dismal truth, evidenced by a massive amount of data, is that college has become divorced from its original mission statement. Once upon a time the goal of university was to help prepare young minds and equip them with the skills required to enter the workforce. Once upon a time, college provided conduits to a well-paying job (as most good jobs once required a college degree). Once upon a time, college was a bridge to a better life!

College Costs Once Were Much Lower

> *"We have a bubble in education, like we had a bubble in housing... College is good for the top 10–15 percent of students. For most others, it's a waste of time and money."*
> **—Peter Thiel, Entrepreneur / Co-founder of PayPal**

Once upon a time, college also used to be affordable to students. For example, in 1973, before the U.S. government started to offer a significant number of college grants, loans, and financial aid, the average cost of college was an order of magnitude lower than it is today!

While exact figures can vary depending on the source, on average public four-year college (in-state) tuition and fees were approximately **$358 per year.** Private four-year colleges were more expensive, with the average tuition and fees around **$1,706 per year.**

But inflation, you say! Surely that must be close to what it is now when you adjust for inflation...? Actually, no—not even close! The 1973 public four-year college cost, adjusted for inflation, would be **$2,536.16/yr** in 2025. And in 1973 the private four-year college would cost **$12,085.70** in 2025 inflation-adjusted dollars.

So, why has the cost of an American college degree gone up by so much? Well, one reason is that the Office of Federal Student Aid (FSA) currently provides around **$114.1 billion** in aid each year to students entering college. This "free money" skews the **College Demand Curve,** pushing it violently to the right. The result is higher and higher tuition each year!

The average cost of college varies by school type, year of study, and location. Below are some average costs for the 2023–2024 school year:

- ☆ Public four-year in-state: $11,260, or $27,146 per year for students living on campus
- ☆ Public four-year out-of-state: $29,150, or $45,708 per year for students living on campus
- ☆ Private nonprofit four-year: $41,540, or $58,628 per year for students living on campus
- ☆ Private colleges: $42,162, or $60,420 per year for students living on campus

Administrative Bloat and Divergence from an Educational Focus

Additionally, universities sadly have become a self-serving artifice that primarily benefits not the students, but the **administration.** As a natural outcome of this, colleges have slowly morphed to become left-leaning bastions of rampant bureaucracy and *mammoth bloat.*

For example, in recent years Yale achieved the unfortunate distinction of having **more administrators and managers than undergraduate students.** For its fewer than five thousand undergraduate students, Yale proudly employs an army of over 5,460 administrators! This trend is only getting worse. It begs the question:

> Who, really, is being served by college under a paradigm where costs are skyrocketing, administrators outnumber the students, and the quality of an average college education is declining rapidly?

Yet the problem is not just limited to bureaucracy and administrative bloat. In fact, these two issues might even be considered "the tip of the iceberg." Far more egregious is the fact that there are numerous examples of immensely wasteful spending by universities on non-educational amenities and decadent "brand" accoutrements.

Perhaps it serves as a "sign of the times" that the stewards of higher education worship at the altar of decadence and over-spending. While simultaneously funding massive multi-million-dollar projects, college administrators quietly usher quality and affordable education to the backseat like a red-headed stepchild.

The bloat I'm referring to always manifests in non-educational expenditures, such as the construction of lavish student centers, large sports stadiums, and other amenities that in no way contribute to the academic mission of these institutions.

Breakdown of College's Pitfalls

What follows are seven salient reasons why a college education—once quite valuable—now no longer makes sense for most people:

1. Skyrocketing Tuition Costs

- **Rising Tuition Fees:** Over the past few decades, the cost of college tuition in the U.S. has risen dramatically, far outpacing inflation and wage growth.

  According to data from the College Board, the average cost of tuition and fees at public four-year institutions has more than tripled since the 1980s. Private college tuition has also seen a significant increase.

- **Cost vs. Value:** As the cost of college rises, the value proposition becomes less favorable. Students and their families are paying more for a degree, but the economic return on that investment has not kept pace, leading many to question whether college is still a good financial decision.

2. Massive Student Debt

- **Student Loan Crisis:** The majority of students now graduate with significant student loan debt. As of 2025, the total student loan debt in the U.S. is over *$1.8136 trillion*, with the average graduate of a private university owing around $42,673 upon graduation.

  This debt burden can take decades to repay, often preventing graduates from saving, buying homes, investing in passive income streams, or starting families.

- **Debt Repayment Challenges:** High levels of student debt can lead to financial strain, especially when graduates struggle to find well-paying jobs.

  The burden of debt can also limit career choices, forcing graduates to take any job that pays enough to cover their loan payments, even if it's not in their field of study or doesn't require a college degree.

3. Underemployment of College Graduates

- ☆ **Low-Paying Jobs:** A growing number of college graduates are finding themselves in jobs that do not require a college degree. According to the Federal Reserve, about *41% of recent college graduates are underemployed*, meaning they work in jobs that typically don't require a bachelor's degree. Many of these jobs offer low wages and limited career advancement opportunities.

- ☆ **Mismatch of Skills and Market Needs:** The labor market has not kept pace with the increasing number of college graduates. Many fields are oversaturated with degree holders, leading to intense competition for a limited number of jobs. Meanwhile, the skills taught in college do not always align with the needs of employers, leaving graduates unprepared for the job market.

4. Questionable ROI (Return on Investment)

- ☆ **Variable Earnings by Degree:** The return on investment for a college degree varies significantly depending on the field of study.

  While degrees in fields like engineering, computer science, or healthcare often lead to high-paying jobs, degrees in humanities, social sciences, or arts may not provide the same financial returns.

  This disparity makes the financial burden of college even harder to justify for many students.

- ☆ **Alternative Pathways:** With the rise of alternative education pathways, such as trade schools, apprenticeships, and online certifications, *many are finding that they can achieve career success without a traditional college degree.*

  These alternatives often come with lower costs, less debt, and quicker entry into the workforce.

5. Changing Perceptions of College Education

- ☆ **Decreased Necessity of a Degree:** Employers are increasingly valuing skills and experience over a college degree. Companies like Google, Apple, and IBM have publicly stated that they *no longer* *require a college degree* for certain positions, focusing instead on what candidates can do.

This shift undermines the traditional notion that a degree is necessary for career success.

- ☆ **Cultural Shifts:** There is a growing cultural recognition that the traditional four-year college route is not the best or only path to success. This has led to a broader acceptance of alternative career paths and a re-evaluation of the societal pressure to attend college.

6. Impact on Quality of Life

- ☆ **Delayed Milestones:** The financial burden of college debt and the challenges of finding well-paying jobs can delay major life milestones such as buying a home, starting a family, or saving for retirement. This delay can have long-term effects on quality of life and financial stability.

- ☆ **Mental and Emotional Strain:** The stress of carrying large amounts of debt and the pressure to find a job that justifies the cost of a degree can take a toll on graduates' mental and emotional well-being. This strain can lead to feelings of regret, frustration, and anxiety about the future.

7. Quality of College Education Is in the Toilet

- ☆ **Shifting Focus:** The unnecessary and caustic shift towards a "customer service" model in higher education has led to decreased academic rigor, with students studying less and grade inflation rising, resulting in graduates who lack depth of knowledge and critical thinking skills.

- ☆ **Inferior "Adjunct" Professors:** The increasing reliance on adjunct faculty and the expansion of online courses have further diminished education quality, as these approaches often fail to provide the same level of student engagement, mentoring, and practical skill development as traditional in-person instruction.

Conclusion: Be a "College Opt-Out"

Run—*don't walk*—from college!

Instead: blow into a few **Warp Whistles.** Consider leveraging funds you might otherwise have spent on college (or had squirreled away for your children's education) and funnel those precious dollars into your IBC Banking policy(ies); then *locate investment opportunities!*

Open a business! Purchase **cash flowing real estate**! Anything would be better than wasting it on college.

For the "mission drift" and administrative bloat in universities is a dismal reminder of what can happen to an organization—even one as stalwart as the learned *university*—when it completely loses sight of its mission and purpose. In this case, college sadly has become nothing but a loadstone for progressive administrators who seek to avoid the real world and live within their collegiate bubbles. The vast majority of administrators (NOT teachers, mind you, but administrators) no longer care to help students learn, grow, or attain valuable job skills; their actions speak far louder than words.

If college administrators actually wanted to help students, they'd instead focus on the **value** and **quality** of the education instead of religiously protecting the *institution* and incentivizing an army of faculty to focus on worthless subjects while at the same time choosing to embrace *ideology over substance.*

More over, the sky-rocketing cost of college education, combined with the burden of student debt and the mismatch between degrees and job market demands, has led many to soundly conclude that college is simply no longer worth its enormous cost.

So, while higher education still offers some benefits, particularly in certain high-demand fields (e.g., STEM), the traditional assumption that a college degree is a guaranteed "ticket to financial security" or that attending college "will yield you higher net worth over your lifetime" is woefully *anachronistic*—a broken relic of a forgotten era.

In short, the promise of college affording students a "better life" is a LIE.

As a matter of fact, college has perhaps become the biggest SCAM in modern history!

IBC

CLOSING REMARKS

LET'S SUMMARIZE ...

Thank you for taking the time to read this book. I hope you found insightful lessons, helpful advice, or at least amusing anecdotes.

The core takeaways of this book are as follows:

- ☆ Learn the **Pyramid of Wealth** and in what Tiers to properly allocate your investments.
- ☆ Study **financial literacy**.
- ☆ **Budget** carefully.
- ☆ **Get out of debt** with alacrity.
- ☆ **Pay yourself first!**
- ☆ Capitalize your **IBC** banking system.
- ☆ Seek **passive investments**.
- ☆ Focus on **PI > ME** with all your passion; track your scorecard.
- ☆ Move from the left to the **right** side of the Cash Flow Quadrant.
- ☆ Legally **avoid taxes** (they're your biggest expense).
- ☆ Don't be afraid to **make deals**. Homeruns are not important; hit as many "singles" and "doubles" as you can.
- ☆ **Avoid college** like the plague! *(and tell your kids to as well!)*

> *Doing the aforementioned actions will get you out of the rat race and allow you to build life-changing* ***generational wealth!***

It has been a pleasure writing these financial advice chapters. May the lessons I shared help you beat the game of life and *warp* you to new levels with all these helpful *financial cheat codes.*

Yours sincerely,

Sean M. Dempsey

Sean Dempsey

FURTHER RESOURCES

If you'd like some valuable resources to get started on your journey, consider these starting points:

- Start reading some or all of the books listed on page xviii.
- Subscribe to the following podcasts:
  - *The Infinite Wealth Podcast* (Anthony Faso and Cameron Christiansen)
  - *Wealth Without Wall Street* (Joey Mure and Russ Morgan)
  - *The Peter Schiff Podcast*
  - *The Lara-Murphy Report (go listen to the first 50 epiodes from the beginning; it's a great deep dive into IBC)*
- Try a *free* version of VYZER for tracking your investments and cash flow. Use this signup link for three months free: **https://vyzer.co/#seandempsey**
- Great personal budgeting software: *Monarch Money* (**www.monarchmoney.com)**
- Great service for starting LLCs: CorpNet (**www.CorpNet.com)**
- Hire a fantastic remote CPA for your business: *New Way Accounting* (**www.newwayaccounting.com)**

APPENDIX

APPLICATION

MY INVESTMENTS, KNOWLEDGE, AND PARTING ADVICE

The best way to build one's financial literacy is to become familiar with **actual investment examples** as well as critical macroeconomic, geopolitical, and financial concepts.

You've just finished reading about eleven financial cheat codes. This book described how to FIND invaluable **Warp Whistles**—and even explained how to PLAY them. However, learning to become proficient with any tool or musical instrument is not theoretical; it's practical! One must study and practice! It's the same with financial **Warp Whistles;** you must take the knowledge in the preceding chapters and put it to work. Go apply what you learned!

Some next steps to build or bolster your financial literacy might be:

- ☆ Go read the books I mentioned in the Introduction.
- ☆ Join (or start) a local investment group.
- ☆ Track how your asset allocations align (or don't) with the target percentages espoused by the **Wealth Pyramid.**
- ☆ Create a **PI > ME** report and associated monthly budget.
- ☆ Schedule a meeting with mentor(s) who have experience with passive investing and/or have established IBC policies.
- ☆ Study REAL WORLD examples of investing passively. You can start this on the next few pages....

Strengthening your financial acumen and learning how to think critically is the act of PRACTICING your Warp Whistles and keeping your instruments in tune.

Yet, note this and note it well: after practice time is over and you've blown into the Whistles, you'll indeed start skipping levels—but **you still need to play the game.** When you do, you're going to fall down. You're going to lose your way. Investing is still a tricky sport. Become battle-tested!

For investing doesn't happen in a test-tube; it happens in the real world! It's a brazen, dirty, dusty, rough-and-tumble, scraped-knees-and-busted-lips sort of sport. If you aren't occasionally left limping or bloodied, you're not playing the game right!

As mentioned at the beginning of this book, your Warp Whistles give you amazing short cuts within the investment landscape, but they are not financial panaceas. This is still real life. We don't live in protective bubbles. You're still going to get beat up and will experience setbacks. You'll have learning curves and challenges. But you need to play the game to win. You can't score a goal when you sit in the bleachers.

So, how about some data to fire you up? What follows is a summary of honest-to-goodness real investments I've made personally so you can analyze them through the same lens in which I view success and failure.

In other words, I will put ALL of the knowledge you have learned so far in this book to the test.

So, before closing the last page on these important topics, let's take a moment to study some real-world examples and look at some of my personal investments, research, and thoughtful financial insights....

MY 2023 PASSIVE INCOME REPORT

What follows is an update I published on December 30, 2023 (and subsequently at the end of 2024), to provide visibility to several investment decisions I had made those years that I wished to recap to my investor group. I believe in an "open kimono" approach when it comes to making investments. Typically you hit singles; sometimes doubles—every once in a while, you knock a grand slam out of the park! Reporting "the good, the bad, and the ugly" is a great way to provide transparency and help others learn and grow!

Friends, Investors, and Colleagues:

I thought it would be fun and enlightening to report on my various prospects, successes, and failures embarked this year. I shall showcase my myriad chaotic financial endeavors undertaken this year.

For context, my investment goals have remained consistent for the last decade: to seek **passive income streams**, so that my Passive Income will ultimately exceed my Monthly Expenses ("PI > ME").

In other words, I choose to define financial freedom not through the lens of attaining some nebulous "pot of gold" in the distant future when I "retire" (using qualified plans such as a 401k, IRA, etc.), but rather through the "here and now" pursuit of purchasing assets that generate consistent streams of passive income.

This paradigm shift from the status quo seeks recurring passive income in a manner far more *prudent* and *safer* than traditional investing.

I'll say one other thing on the topic: I don't choose to conflate investing with throwing money in the stock market and hoping for the best (aka "speculating").

Although I fully admit that certain equities with a solid track record of many decades can sometimes be prudent investments—when they pay consistent dividends—yet even they are subject to the macro trends of a mercurial marketplace as well as the vicious whims of the "market cycle." Even a stock market speculator theoretically gaining that coveted "10% average return each year" (hint: this is a myth!) can still wake up one day to find more than half of their nest egg wiped out by a massive bust that "no one saw coming!"

My 2023 Investment Scorecard

Anyway, without further pontificating, here are my passive investing pursuits for 2023 along with a very brief narrative about their relative success or failure:

#1 - Lobster Boat and Commercial Lobster Fishing Business				
Investment	**Cash Flow**	**Financed By**	**% Equity**	**Tier**
$163,103.00	$2,500+/wk lobster sales	IBC Policy Loan (Tier 1 Capital)	25%	4

Fisher Lobster, LLC—Lobster Startup Business (Speculating)

- ☆ **Opportunity:** This was an interesting opportunity I just couldn't pass up. Admittedly, this is one of the wilder and more speculative pursuits I have ever engaged in. Why? Because I know absolutely nothing about lobstering! And I know even less about buying and maintaining large commercial fishing boats. However, what made this deal enticing (and thus worth pursuing) was the operator! If the secret to successful real estate investing is location, location, location—then the secret to a successful passive business investment is operator, operator, operator!

  Without making a long story even longer, I have known my lobstering partner for over a decade. He has over 20 years' experience lobstering. So, over a beer (or two ... or even three) I learned that "all he needed was a much bigger boat" as well as some capital for investing in new lobster gear (rope, new traps, etc.). After even more beers ... a business arrangement was born!

He'd captain the boat and haul the lobster; I'd provide all the capital. And we'd split the business 25/75 (me/him). Most importantly: he would be 100% responsible for everything. Voilà! Passive investment in a burgeoning lobstering business.

☆ **Results:** So far, so good! While it was a wild ride at the beginning (e.g., the boat had over $24,000 in repairs right off the bat!), ever since then it has been relatively "smooth sailing"—with the business hauling between 500–1,000 lobsters each week (weather-permitting!) We sell most of them wholesale at an average of ~$6.75/lb.

The nascent net income in 2023 ($22,152.70 NOI, imputing a **13.58%** COC return) I feel is just the beginning for the business since it's in its very first year (hell, most businesses take a **loss** in their first 3 years!). One goal we have for 2024 is to sell more of our lobsters at retail prices—directly to restaurants or local seafood lovers. That'll increase profit margin by over 35%. Our value proposition is this: we'll deliver the lobsters right to you (as long as you're within a 25-mile radius); no one else on the seacoast is offering anything like that. So, it's time to be "shellfish," and make some real money!

COC Return: 13.58%

#2 - ATM Investing—Managed Fund				
Investment	**Cash Flow**	**Financed By**	**% Equity**	**Tier**
$104,000.00	$2,262/mo	IBC Policy Loan (Tier 1 Capital)	100%	4

Prestige Fund D VI—ATM Fund (Speculating)

- **Opportunity:** In 2022, I speculated in an ATM Fund after listening to a terrific, educational podcast on the topic. Based on this success, I doubled down in 2023. Many Managed Funds are Tier 3; however, I feel this is Tier 4 asset because I have **no control** of the underlying assets (the ATMs) and also due to my lack of familiarity with this space (see "Laws of Gold" in Chapter 4).

  Still, this is a bit more "boring" investment vehicle than others this year. However, the results are consistent. And, most importantly, it's **100% passive!** I receive funds ACH'ed into my checking account like clockwork on the 23rd of each month for the next 7 years.

- **Results:** Aside from being a great COC return **(26.10%)**, the asset class also boasts terrific **tax benefits!**

  The investor can write off the ENTIRE asset as a depreciable asset against their taxable income in year one ("bonus depreciation"). This allows me to save tens of thousands of dollars in taxes each year for each ATM fund in which I invest. I love these ATM funds and will continue to put money in them each year.

COC Return: 26.10%

#3 - Short Term Rental Fund—Managed Fund				
Investment	Cash Flow	Financed By	% Equity	Tier
$50,000.00	$145/qtr (dividend)	IBC Policy Loan (Tier 1 Capital)	100%	3

TVR 2 LLC, A-2 Tier, Techvestor STR Fund—TVR 2 LLC (Investing)

- **Opportunity:** In May 2023, I invested $50K in a managed fund that purchases and manages short-term rental units. I took out a "flyer" on this fund. I recognize I already am over-exposed to the short-term rental asset class! But given I know quite a bit about STRs, I felt it was worthwhile trying to make short-term rental investing even more **passive** than it already is for me.
- **Results:** Thus far, results have been uninspiring. Since May 2023 there has been only one (1) distribution of $145.00 (in November 2023). I trust this to improve greatly in 2024. I also understand there will be a sale of the asset(s) at a profit within five years; but regardless, I most likely will not be investing further in this fund. It's too little juice (i.e., meager cash flow) and not worth the squeeze.
- **Brass tacks:** stay away from this one!

COC Return: 0.29%

#4 - Oil and Gas Investing—Managed Fund				
Investment	**Cash Flow**	**Financed By**	**% Equity**	**Tier**
$100,000.00	$157-167/mo (dividend)	IBC Policy Loan (Tier 1 Capital)	100%	4

King Operating Partners II LP, Oil and Gas Fund (Speculation)

- ☆ **Opportunity:** I invested in an Oil + Gas fund in January 2023 to take advantage of the incredible tax benefits and massive upside potential in this space.

  This is one of the more ***speculative*** investments I've made in recent years, and the jury is most definitely still out as to whether or not it will pay off. It could very well be a massive flop ... or a spectacular windfall. The results will be entirely dependent on a) the price of oil [and if it appreciates], b) the ability of the drilled wells to strike oil, and c) the ability of the fund manager(s) to sell the assets for a significant profit in year 5.

- ☆ **Results:** I made my investment in January 2023. Cash flow did not start "flowing" (pun intended) until September—nearly 8 months later. So far, the cash flow has been anemic. BUT that's frankly to be expected in the first 12-18 months (any cash flow for this asset class during this early period is just gravy!). The goal of this investment class is to strike oil, start massive production, and then sell the oil-producing well(s) to a far bigger player (e.g., Mobil, BP, etc.) at 10-20X+ the CAPEX + drilling costs. So, I'll know ~ year 2027/2028 if my investment will 3-10x OR—if it even breaks even. It'll be a fun ride!

COC Return: 0.66% (thus far)

#5 - Buyout of Partner in Marketing Agency				
Investment	**Cash Flow**	**Financed By**	**% Equity**	**Tier**
$176,400.00	N/A	Promissory Note paid down by cash flow	85%	2

Loud Canvas Media, LLC—Digital Marketing Agency (Investing)

- **Opportunity:** In January of 2023 I choose to buy out a minority stake interest from a silent partner in my web and digital marketing business, Loud Canvas Media. My previous partner held 10.00% (a deal coordinated in 2020 for an exchange in equity in his business).

  After much thought and prayer, I decided early on this year that the BEST thing I could do with my money from an investment perspective was not to put too much of it in speculative asset classes but rather invest in myself and my primary "B"usiness. In other words, I know my ability to grow and expand my own business. So, I chose to be jealous of its equity and its growth potential. I've found over the years that the best investment I can make is **"invest in myself,"** so this was my way of doing that.

  I coordinated a plan to pay him out on an installment plan over 84 months at $2,100.00/mo.

- **Results:** The long-term results of this decision will pan out over the next decade or so. But so far, since executing the buyout, the agency has already grown by **13.78%.** Through hiring a new CEO/president (last year) as well his focus on opening new strategic verticals and building strong partnerships, I hope to grow the company by 10–15% YOY for the next 10+ years—which would make this equity buyout perhaps one of the best investments of my career! Time will tell....

COC Return: TBD

#6 - Real Estate—Lakehouse in Milton NH (STR)				
Investment	**Cash Flow**	**Financed By**	**% Equity**	**Tier**
$500,000.00	Loss of ($-27,706)	IBC Policy Loan (Tier 1 Capital)	33.33%	3

JASK Properties, LLC—STR Company (Investing)

- ☆ **Opportunity:** In August 2023 I went into business with several of my best friends. (NB: Going into business with friends is often problematic; but I choose my partners very carefully and believe I have made the right decision here with intelligent, hard working, and very solid partners.) The opportunity is another short-term rental (STR) property in New Hampshire. Having managed and run short-term rentals in the area now for over 10 years, I am very familiar with the business model, the pitfalls, the challenges, and the potential for exciting upside/success.

  This specific property offered a unique opportunity in that it is an absolutely beautiful lake house (fully renovated) and is essentially **"turn-key."** Moreso, it is situated directly on a private lake and boasts over 200 ft of sandy beachfront. (PS No others on the entire lake have anything else like it.)

  I believe the sellers misclassified the listing and sold the property 20–25% cheaper than they should have (i.e., they listed it on the MLS themselves, without an agent, and without checking the "lakefront property" box). This afforded my partners and me an "opportunity of a lifetime" once we noticed the listing! Not giving the sellers an opportunity to determine their mistake, we immediately offered $1.5M cash and closed the deal within a few weeks (and requested ALL furniture in the home to be included as part of the sale). I sourced my ⅓ share of the funds for the deal through IBC policy loans, as I do with all my strategic investments. This allowed the deal to close quickly and without a commercial bank involved.

☆ Results:

- **Cons:** In 2023 the business was NOT profitable (nearly a $30K taxable loss); BUT this is due to CAPEX we invested in a brand-new hot tub, electrical work, a new patio, and a new 100 gal hot water tank.
- **Pros:** I listed the property for rent on Airbnb BEFORE we had even closed the deal and purchased the home (haha, in retrospect this was very foolish). We closed on August 10 and had the place rented on Airbnb the week after! We were able to rent every remaining weekend in August and September for between $4,000–$6,500 a weekend! Given our property is a lake house, we plan to make most of our revenues in the summer; that said, we have had preliminary success renting it in the fall and winter. I am very encouraged by our ability to attain banner results in 2024! We also did a **cost segregation study** on this property to take maximum advantage of the asset from a tax/depreciation perspective.

COC Return: N/A (not yet profitable)

#7 - Real Estate—Multi-Family Rental in Manchester NH				
Investment	Cash Flow	Financed By	% Equity	Tier
$150,000.00	TBD	Debt @ 8.00%	50.00%	2

305 Cedar LLC—9-Unit Multi-Family Rental (Investing)

☆ **Opportunity:** In December 2023 my lovely wife and I purchased a multi-family rental property in Manchester, New Hampshire, with nine (9) units. The goal will be to progressively increase rents and refinance after two years (optionally pulling out equity) once the commercial asset has appreciated accordingly. In the meantime, the asset will generate a very comfortable cash flow. I am most encouraged that this investment will be entirely passive, given our friend and business partner, Tim Baxter (and his property management company), shall be driving the day-to-day execution of the asset.

☆ **Results:** We closed on the property only December 28, 2023, so the jury is still very much out on this one. However, there is a very solid pro forma promising strong results of $61,298.00/yr net profit (in the first year) and then after rent revisions, increasing up from there.

My wife and I are 50% equity stakeholders, so we plan on receiving roughly $2,500–3,000/mo, imputing a COC Return of 20.43% (in the first year). Time will tell what the long-term results will be....

COC Return: N/A (not yet profitable)

#8 - Private Loans to Colleagues, Friends, and Businesses				
Investment	**Cash Flow**	**Financed By**	**% Equity**	**Tier**
$285,000.00	32.78% ($7,786/mo)	IBC Policy Loan (Tier 1 Capital)	N/A	3

Private Loans to Colleagues, Friends, and Businesses (Investing)

☆ **Opportunity:** With stagnant cash value (CV) available in my IBC policies, I choose to loan monies out, whenever possible, to worthy and reliable persons that represent a low credit risk.

- These individuals were not "bankable" due to a variety of reasons. Or sometimes they needed money faster than would be possible through a standard banking instrument.

☆ **Results:** Loans with an average rate of return of **32.78%** have resulted in passive income of just under $8k/mo.

#9 - CAPEX in Owned Rental Property (Short Term Rentals)				
Investment	Cash Flow	Financed By	% Equity	Tier
$43,426.00	NA	STR Cash Flow	100%	2

Dempsey Estates—Refurbish Properties to Increase Value (Investing)

- ☆ **Opportunity:** Leveraging cash flow produced by short-term property assets, in 2023 I invested in CAPEX to improve the buildings and interior of properties at Somersworth, New Hampshire, as well as Morristown, Vermont (aka "Maple House Manor", "MHM").

  Specifically, for Somersworth, I invested ~$13K installing a standalone "whole home" generator on site, which will turn on whenever there is a loss of power. This will improve the ability for the asset to perform during the winter if/when weather causes a loss of power. I also invested $7,500 in new wood floors throughout the 2nd floor of the home. Additionally, I invested $10K for indoor pool repairs and improvements at MHM. I also invested an additional $15K finishing the basement in MHM, turning it into a beautiful game room for guest use/enjoyment.

- ☆ **Results:** The impact of these capital expenditures will be hard to quantify in the short term; however, over the long-term, I expect the results to manifest in a greater number of five-star reviews as well as an increased number of stays. The CAPEX has also improved the underlying value of the real estate assets themselves.

COC Return: N/A

Other items of note:

- ☆ I sold off my business *Remnant Properties LLC* via a long-term promissory note. Ultimately, this business (land flipping) was one I regret getting involved in—not because I don't appreciate the business model, but because I failed to acknowledge the very active involvement and regular commitment required.
  - In 2023 I re-learned that the TYPE of investment paradigms best suited to an investor's "investor DNA" is so crucial during the early phases of investing. It's so tempting to want to just throw money at fun and exciting ideas (especially if the returns look promising). But I learned (the hard way) that this is not the best way to proceed. Learn from me and don't make the same mistake!
  - I sold this business (at a fraction of its real long-term value) to two people I love; I know they will run the business far, far better than I did. And I know they will recognize a lot more long-term value and profit in the business than I achieved.

LOOKING INTO 2024 ...

Some goals going into the new year (2024) include:

- ☆ Investing marketing dollars in growing my fairly new business, ManagedBNB, LLC, and doubling its revenues and profits in 2024.
- ☆ Increasing profitability of Maple House Manor and reducing by 15–20% unnecessary operational spend and overhead (e.g., reduced contractor spend, invest in solar panels to decrease my $1,500+/mo electric bill).
- ☆ Several private loans made in 2023 mature in 2024; realize these profits and reinvest....
- ☆ Grow Industrial Traffic's top line revenue and increase profitability through partnership with cost-conscious operators and strategic partners.
- ☆ Look into investing in more ATM funds to increase passive income from that asset class.
- ☆ Evaluate additional private loans to colleagues and small businesses (ideally at rates of 15%+ APR).
- ☆ Focus on growth of JASK Properties LLC and its summer rental income. Ideally, bring on an operator by the end of this year or early next year to manage day-to-day management of the short-term rental.

PRO TIP

I didn't just pull the numbers above out of a hat. I believe very strongly in TRACKING success and failure and being completely honest with the results. Smarter people than I have said, "What you track grows; what you track and report on grows exponentially."

To this end, I found an absolutely wonderful piece of online software called **Vyzer**. It allows investors to track their success and transactional history in various investment classes, including business assets, real estate assets, managed funds, and even personal loans. It provides a terrific cash flow management tool for forecasting purposes. It'll inform you if you're missing a monthly distribution as well as provide guidance on what your IRR and ROI metrics are per investment. It's free to sign up. Give it a try: ***https://vyzer.co/#seandempsey***. I recommend it highly!

MY 2024 PASSIVE INCOME REPORT

This appendix item is meant to *complement* the preceding report of my 2023 investments (which was admittedly a bit overly-aggressive). In 2024 my focus was back on my "bread and butter" Tier 2 (Multi-family Real Estate) assets.

#1 - Real Estate—Multi-Family Rental in Farmington NH				
Investment	**Cash Flow**	**Financed By**	**% Equity**	**Tier**
$40,000.00	$312.79/mo (thus far)	IBC Policy Loan (Tier 1 Capital)	18.75%	2

11 Orange LLC—5-Unit Multi-Family Rental (Investing)

- ☆ **Opportunity:** In May 2024 my wife and I again invested with Timothy Baxter; we purchased equity in a five (5) unit multi-family rental property in Farmington, New Hampshire. The business model involves progressively increasing rents to get them to market rates and then refinance within two years or less so that the original capital ($50K) will be returned. In the meantime, the asset will generate consistent cash flow.
- ☆ **Results:** We closed on the property May 2, 2024, so the jury is still out on this one. However, we are actively in the process of refinancing the property to extricate our original investment funds (well before the 24-month mark)! There is also a solid pro forma promising results of $34,457/yr cash flow once rents are fully stabilized.

Since we are 18.75% equity stakeholders, we should receive roughly $538.39/mo in cash flow (per the pro forma). Prior to refinancing, this imputes a COC return of **12.92%.** Once we get our original $50K investment returned to us (as early as within the first month of 2025), our **COC Return** essentially becomes infinite. And we will continue to receive ~$530/mo cash flow in perpetuity after having our entire principal back in full! So far, the rents have not fully stabilized; as such, we have just seen $312.79/mo materialize to date.

Projected COC Return: 12.92% (once stabilized)

Actual COC Return: 9.38% (thus far)

Projected COC Return within 3 Months: Infinite!

#2 - Real Estate—Multi-Family Rentals in Multiple Towns				
Investment	**Cash Flow**	**Financed By**	**% Equity**	**Tier**
$200,000.00	$1,194/mo (thus far)	IBC Policy Loan (Tier 1 Capital)	12.7497%	2

IG 55U LLC—55-Unit Multi-Family Rental (Investing)

☆ **Opportunity:** In July 2024 my wife and I invested in a sizable multi-family real estate opportunity, along with around 25 other persons from our "Investor Guild," which I founded (i.e., an investment club hosted at my house).

Once again, we invested with real estate magnate, Timothy Baxter. We purchased 12.7497% stake of *55 total units* across four (4) different rental properties in New Hampshire.

As per three of the "5 Rules of Gold" defined by Clason (see Chapter 4), we invested our money with an operator *we personally know and trust* in an asset class *we know well and understand*, and in a geographic location right in our backyard.

*"**Rules of Gold (Reminder from Chapter 4):***
***Rule #3:** Gold clings to the protection of the person who invests their gold with wise people.*

***Rule #4:** Gold slips away from the person who invests gold into purposes through which they are not familiar."*
—George Clason, Richest Man in Babylon

Again, the goal of this particular investment schema is to take on a large number of Section-8 renters (as well as progressively increase non-Section-8 rents) and then refinance within two years or less so that the original capital ($200K) can be returned in full!

In the meantime, the asset will generate a consistent cash flow; it will also appreciate in value by virtue of rents being increased—simply by assuming the same original **CAP rate** as when the asset was purchased.

☆ Results:

- We closed on the property July 2, 2024, so only a few months of initial rental income have occurred.
- The pro forma promises strong results of $296,200/yr cash flow once rents are stabilized.
- Since my wife and I are 12.7497% equity stakeholders, we should eventually receive roughly $3,189.09/mo post-stabilization.
- Prior to refinancing, this imputes a COC return of 19.13%.
- Once we get our original $200K investment returned to us (within 24 months or less), our COC return becomes infinite while the monthly cash flow will decrease slightly.

☆ Worth noting is that in the very first month of this investment, it returned a (pre-stabilization) net profit, which is extremely rare for deals of this size and nature!

☆ My wife and I received pro rata cash flow of $1,194.14 starting end of July 2024. Having only purchased the property in early July, we found this very encouraging. Even if this monthly return stayed as is and did not grow (which is unlikely), it would still impute a 7.16% COC Return.

Projected COC Return: 19.13% (once stabilized)

Actual COC Return 7.16% (thus far)

Projected COC Return within 24 Months: Infinite!

#3 - Real Estate—Multi-Family Rentals in Multiple NH Towns				
Investment	**Cash Flow**	**Financed By**	**% Equity**	**Tier**
$22,500.00	N/A (yet)	IBC Policy Loan (Tier 1 Capital)	7.222%	2

330 Central LLC—36-Unit Multi-Family Rental (Investing)

☆ **Opportunity:** In late August 2024 my wife and I again invested in a sizable multi-family real estate opportunity, along with roughly eight additional persons from our "Investor Guild."

This was yet another Timothy Baxter deal. We purchased a 7.222% stake in 36 units from several different rental properties in New Hampshire. This deal also carries with it a cute little "cherry on top" in that there is a 3-unit which will be split off and sold—expediting some return of capital to the investors.

☆ **Results:**

- As this deal just closed (weeks ago, as of the writing of this report), it is too soon to post actual results.
- However, if the pro forma is accurate, there will be a $212,174/yr pre-tax net income.
- Given our share of 7.222%, this imputes a $15,323.20/yr passive cash flow, or $1,276.93/mo. That's a **68.10% COC return!**

- And, once again, the COC return should become infinite once the business plan fully executes, and the property is refinanced (within two years or less)—returning 100% of investor capital back.
- Note: I did need to guarantee the debt in order to negotiate for a few extra percentage points on this deal. This admittedly increases my risk (in a calculated fashion).

COC Return: 68.10% (once stabilized)

Actual COC Return: N/A (thus far)

Projected COC Return within 24 Months: Infinite!

#4—Real Estate—BRRRR in Memphis TN				
Investment	**Cash Flow**	**Financed By**	**% Equity**	**Tier**
$29,939.33	N/A (yet)	IBC Policy Loan (Tier 1 Capital)	33.33%	2

2100 Stovall—Fully-Managed BRRRR Rental (Investing)

☆ **Opportunity:** Two good friends and I teamed up once again to invest. The three of us have done multiple deals together. Perhaps unconsciously, we choose to affirm the wise African proverb:

"If you want to go fast, go alone;
if you want to go far, go together."

In this case, the opportunity is simple: buy a rental property to rehab, fix it up, refinance it (and get the initial capital back within 6 months), rent it out, receive ongoing cash flow in perpetuity. In other words, a "BRRRR" stands for "Buy, Rehab, Refinance, Rent, Repeat."

The best part of the entire deal is that a management company in Tennessee manages the entire process—from soup to nuts. We just provide the initial seed capital.

As such, the opportunity seemed too good to pass up. And while it's not exactly in "our backyard," as I often prefer with real estate deals, I felt the risk was low given the successful (and well vetted) track record of the operator (the management company).

☆ **Results:** This deal closed in late August 2024, so results won't be known for 5-6 more months. However, EXPECTED cash flow is *$848.23/mo* AFTER we get 100% of our invested capital back in a refinance.

Cash Flow After Refinance: $848.23/mo

($281.08/mo is my 1/3 portion)

Projected COC Return within 6 Months: Infinite!

#5 - Oil and Gas Investing—Managed Fund				
Investment	**Cash Flow**	**Financed By**	**% Equity**	**Tier**
+$150,000.00	$1,443.42/mo (dividend)	IBC Policy Loan (Tier 1 Capital)	100%	4

King Operating Partners II LP, Oil and Gas Fund (Speculation)

☆ **Opportunity:** I doubled down and re-invested in the same Oil + Gas fund as I did in 2023—this time with another $150K investment. I am very bullish on oil and gas given the current inflationary period of our macroeconomic landscape. I also wished to take advantage of the incredible tax benefits that this investment class affords.

☆ **Tax Benefits:** I was effectively able to *avoid* having to write a $45,000 check to the IRS (for my quarterly 'Estimated Taxes') in June 2024. Because I wrote a check for $150,000 to this managed fund, one might think I went the wrong direction (only a fool spends $150K to save $45K, right?). However, in addition to providing consistent monthly cash flow, the +$150K is an investment that ultimately may pay 3–5X+ the invested capital (admittedly this is Tier 4/*Speculation*!) That said, the U.S. government would brazenly be using the pilfered $45K to help fund illegal and unconstitutional proxy wars in Ukraine with my money (or give it to Israel). So, in many ways NOT paying the government its extortion fee ("blood money") puts my conscience at ease. And that's ... just priceless.

- ☆ **Results:** So far, I am in $250K total on this fund between 2023 and 2024. I do not plan to invest more until the "chickens come home." Please read my commentary on this investment in my 2023 Passive Income Report. I won't repeat myself here. However, I will say that my passive income has gone from less than ~$200/mo (in 2023) to averaging $1,443.42/mo. And it seems to be progressively growing each month. Again, that's just the "cherry on top."

Future COC Return: 5.88% (prior to sale of asset)

Actual COC Return: 3.98% (2024)

Projected ROI by 2026: 100%–300%

#6—UPDATE—ATM Investing—Managed Fund				
Original Investment	**Cash Flow**	**Financed By**	**% Equity**	**Tier**
$208,000.00 (total invested)	$0.00/mo!	IBC Policy Loan (Tier 1 Capital)	100%	4

Prestige Fund D VI—ATM Fund (Speculating)

- ☆ **Opportunity:** See 2023 Passive Income Report

☆ **Results:** Bad news bears on this investment's front. For more than a year and a half I was receiving $2,262/mo like clockwork (from each of my two funds, totaling to $4,524/mo). Then—all of a sudden—*the deposits stopped!*

I knew something was amiss when my **Vyzer** online software (which I highly recommend, by the way) informed me the two monthly cash flow deposits were both late. I emailed into the fund advisor and within a day got a disturbing notice: without warning, the fund was arbitrarily moving away from monthly distributions to quarterly distributions.

I wasn't a big fan of this, to say the least; but life being what it is, and there being only so many things one can make a stink over, I decided not to let this be a hill to die on. The next distribution would be in another two (2) months and would be the sum of 3 months' worths of ATM dividends. Okay, fine. I can live with that....

Only, when two months came and went *with no distribution*, I began to worry. Now, I smelled a rat!

Suffice it to say, without going into the sordid details, it appears that the operating company for the ATMs, Paramount, suddenly decided—for reasons still unknown—not to live up to the terms of the fund contract and began withholding payments to all investors!

So, in August 2024, investors in the ATM funds filed a lawsuit against Heller Capital Group, the parent company of Paramount, to gain control of the ATM network. The investors (of which I am a party) claim that Heller Capital Group failed to pay over $65 million in fees since April 2024.

We investors are naturally concerned that the ATMs are in danger, and that the network going down could put ~$700 million at risk.

The majority of the ATMs are located in convenience stores. As testified in court, the lawsuit was filed to prevent the network from being ruined, and to protect their ATM businesses and business opportunities.

So, in the realm of "minor annoyances" to "total stink-bombs," this investment has made a sharp left turn squarely into the latter camp.

To be clear, the lawyers believe that real assets do exist; ideally the court system will prevail. Some or all investor monies will be returned.

That said, I remain skeptical I will receive my initial investment back in full. I am of course hopeful, but not confident in any way.

I still am hesitant to throw around the word "Ponzi scheme" too early, but this entire debacle has opened my eyes to the critical importance of personally knowing or doing proper due diligence on the **OPERATOR** of any passive investment.

To share my failure here, I simply did not do enough due diligence! I fell into the same trap that I warned about in this very book: *becoming complacent due to "the safety in numbers."* Clearly, that did not help me here. There are ~2700 other investors (across 25 funds) at risk of losing FAR more money than me; but "misery loves company" is no real solace.

I must admit, this situation has soured me to future investing in managed funds as an asset class (at least without SIGNIFICANT due diligence going forward).

It really is a bummer, because this asset class checked all the boxes for me (passive return, massive depreciation in year 1 and tax write-off, "mailbox money," etc.).

This situation also made me better understand that if I can't TOUCH it and FEEL it with my own eyes, I should be hesitant. But, again, the chief issue here was the operator. The CEO of Paramount—a man named Daryl Heller—appears to be a royal scumbag and charlatan. Were there warning signs, or did the 'set it and forget it' nature of this investment blind me (and the other investors?) I do not exactly know....

Current Cash Flow: $0.00/mo (bad news bears)

Current IRR: 13.41% (Fund 1 and Fund 2 averaged)

#7—UPDATE—STR Fund—Managed Fund				
Original Investment	**Cash Flow**	**Financed By**	**% Equity**	**Tier**
$50,000.00	$738.69/qtr	IBC Policy Loan (Tier 1 Capital)	100%	3

TVR 2 LLC, A-2 Tier, Techvestor STR Fund—TVR 2 LLC (Investing)

- ☆ **Opportunity:** See 2023 Passive Income Report
- ☆ **Results:** I may have been a bit hasty judging this fund too harshly in my 2023 report. While I feel it's still an uninspiring investment—and I also feel it gives me a lack of flexibility and control—still, it, in theory, has some collateral and long-term potential.

  Its cash flows also picked up quite a bit since my first report. Here have been my distributions thus far:

  - February 12, 2024—$514.48
  - May 6, 2024—$1,046.19
  - August 19, 2024—$893.49
  - November 20, 2024—$500.59

  All in all, still rather anemic (compared to what I can get with other passive investments). I still won't likely be investing any more in this fund or others like it.

COC Return: 5.90%

Projected COC Return: 6.54%

#8—UPDATE—Commercial Lobster Fishing Business				
Original Investment	**Cash Flow**	**Financed By**	**% Equity**	**Tier**
$163,103.00 (nothing added)	$1,000/mo distribution	IBC Policy Loan (Tier 1 Capital)	25%	4

Fisher Lobster, LLC—Lobster Startup Business (Speculation)

☆ **Opportunity:** See 2023 Passive Income Report.

☆ **Results:** Treacherous—just like the high seas! To date this is one of my most speculative and treacherous investments.

As mentioned more than a few times in this book, startup businesses are inherently risky. In fact, the vast majority of businesses fail in their first three years. That said, I personally know and completely trust the OPERATOR in this business—and that made the opportunity worth it for me. See 2023 Passive Income Report for more info.

So, what were the results in 2024? Well, cash flow has declined significantly to be honest.

Whereas at times in 2023 we were cash-flowing as much as $4,000/wk, in 2024 most of that cash flow dried up.

Why? Two primary reasons:

- Bad Catch. In short, the pesky lobsters just stopped crawling into the dang traps! Call it (lack of) luck, fate, or the wrath of an angry sea god—but, for whatever reason, this was apparently one of the WORST lobstering seasons in recent memory.
- And that's not just me saying this; this is just a "known truth" down at the New Hampshire docks. The collective pack of seamen are all scratching their heads and shaking their fists at Poseidon!
- Boat woes! Our boat has had a myriad of issues in 2024. In Q2 the boat had to be hauled out of the water for a complete tune-up and lengthy list of repairs.

- For starters, the propellor had to be completely rebuilt. The hydraulics had issues. The bottom fiberglass right rudder came completely unhinged and needed to be rebuilt. We needed to completely repaint the hull (with waterproof paint—which ain't cheap). The list just went on and on....

The old boater's adage is quite germane:

The two happiest days of a boater's life are when you buy the boat and when you sell the boat....

Long story short, the entire year provided only $5,000 in total cash flow to me. For the third quarter (until Sept. 15), we had a net loss and thus had to cease distributions ("cash flows") while we took on debt to pay for boat repairs.

Only in November 2024 were my partner and I able to resume some sort of distribution from the business profits.

Based on the pro forma for the remainder of the year's projected revenues, I am planning to take $1,000/mo as a guaranteed payment (GP) beginning in 2025. If this remains consistent, it imputes a COC return of 7.35%. Could be worse, I suppose.

We shall see what 2025 looks like...

Actual 2024 COC Return: 3.07%

(given bad first 3 quarters due to boat repairs)

Projected COC Return in 2025: 7.35%

#9—UPDATE—Multi-Family Rental in Manchester NH				
Original Investment	**Cash Flow**	**Financed By**	**% Equity**	**Tier**
$150,000.00 (nothing added)	$1,236.49/mo	Debt @ 8.00%	50.00%	2

305 Cedar LLC—9-Unit Multi-Family Rental (Investing)

☆ **Opportunity:** See 2023 Passive Income Report.

☆ **Results:** In 2023 there was no cash flow because the asset was purchased in December 2023.

In 2024 the cash flows have been:

- $785.00 (Jan.) [plus $8,400 return of capital]
- $515.00 (Feb.)
- $2,000.00 (Mar.)
- $1,161.05 (Apr.)
- $534.06 (May.)
- $488.56 (Jun.)
- $1,574.40 (Jul.)
- $1,562.66 (Aug.)
- $1,998.24 (Sept.)
- $1,043.66 (Oct.)
- $1,335.97 (Nov.)
- $1,839.34 (Dec.)

☆ The average monthly cash flow is $1,236.49 (disregarding the $8.4K). The total net cash flow in 2024 was **$23,237.94.**

☆ This imputes a COC Return of **15.49%**

COC Return: 15.49%

(Jan 01 2024 - Dec 311, 2024)

Projected COC for 2025: 20.43%

(based on stabilizing rents)

#10 - UPDATE—Lakehouse in Milton NH (STR)				
Original Investment	**Cash Flow**	**Financed By**	**% Equity**	**Tier**
$500,000.00 (nothing added)	$2,910/mo	IBC Policy Loan (Tier 1 Capital)	33.33%	3

JASK Properties, LLC—STR Company (Investing)

☆ **Opportunity:** See 2023 Passive Income Report.

☆ **Results:**

- In 2023 (first year of operation) there was a -$30K loss.
- In 2024 there was a net profit of **$104,761.16!** And that's including $22K in unbudgeted CAPEX invested in the property for HVAC improvements (new mini-splits).
- **$34.9K/yr cash flow** for each 1/3 partner—or $2,910/mo.

COC Return: 6.98%

Projected COC in 2025: ~8.50%

(assumes no unbudgeted CAPEX and same number of stays as in 2024)

Notable Item for Consideration in 2025:

My JASK partners and I were hasty/impetuous and did NOT use leverage when making the initial real estate purchase. This is why COC Return numbers are low. In other words, there is NO MORTAGE in place; we paid cash to secure this property (dumb!).

If interest rates come down in 2025, I will gently advise my partners to consider financing this asset with a "cash-out refi;" the net profits of the property can support a mortgage payment, and this simple action will significantly improve the COC Return of the investment by 1.5X-3X+.

For example, let's assume long-term fixed interest rates actually stay where they are now (~6.20%). If we finance our $1.5M asset with 20% "down" (equity portion not financed), it imputes a loan of $1.20M and a mortgage payment of $7,354/mo. This modifies the invested capital (the "cash outlay") from $500K each investor to $100K/each. Let's look what this will do to the key metrics for this Tier 3 investment:

- The projected 2025 cash flow of the asset is $124K/yr ($10,333/mo). This assumes no $22K+ unbudgeted CAPEX and the same number of reservations in 2025 as in 2024. Subtracting the mortgage ($7,354/mo) leaves a cash flow of $2,979/mo.
- Each partner's ⅓ share of that is now $11,916/yr ($993/mo).
- Thus, the simple act of adding a mortgage increases the COC Return for each investor from **6.98%** to **11.92%!**
- AND each investor would get a check for **$400K** handed to them—**to be used on other passive investments!**
- While taking on just a bit more risk (e.g., the STR rental market could, in theory, slow down vs. stay consistent), this simple step seems very much like a "no-brainer"—especially if the interest rate environment improves (lowers) in 2025.

LOOKING INTO 2025 ...

Some goals going into 2025 include:

- ☆ Continue investing marketing dollars into growing my property management Business, ManagedBNB, LLC, and doubling its cash flows in 2025.
- ☆ Evaluate the success of the Memphis BRRRR investment strategy and reinvest further, if successful.
- ☆ Refinance JASK Properties LLC's primary real estate asset (if partner consensus permits).
- ☆ Determine viability of managing and marketing a nascent investment fund.
- ☆ Grow personal network; raise significant capital for multi-family real estate investment opportunities in which I'm a part.
- ☆ Divest from several STR properties (an asset class in which I am overweight); I feel this is very prudent given the *coming collapse* of multiple financial markets.
- ☆ *Write more books...?*

MY 2025 PASSIVE INCOME REPORT

As a follow-up to my 2024 Passive Income Report, what follows is an update on all passive investments made in 2023 and 2024, and their success during the 2025 calendar year (as well as a few new investments):

#1 - Real Estate—Multi-Family Rental in Farmington, NH				
Capital Invested	**Cash Flow**	**Financed By**	**% Equity**	**Tier**
$50,000 (less $40,559.16 returned) = $9,440.84	$304.21/mo	IBC Policy Loan (Tier 1 Capital)	18.75%	2

11 Orange LLC—5-Unit Multi-Family Rental (Tier 2—Investing)

- ☆ **Opportunity:** See *2024 Passive Income Report*
- ☆ **Results:** In 2025, $40,559.16 was returned (of the original $50,000 principal invested). That represents 81.12% of the original capital returned in 2025 (originally invested on April 25, 2024). From a COC perspective, this leaves $9,440.84 of original outlay remaining. With an imputed $304.21/mo cash flow maintained ($3,650.52/yr) the COC return is 38.67%.
- ☆ **Note:** there is an expected "second bite at the apple" in 2026 as rent stabilization continues to improve. A second strategic refi may be possible, allowing the remaining capital invested to be returned while maintaining consistent cash flow.

COC Return: 38.67%

#2 - Real Estate – Multi-Family Rentals in Multiple Towns				
Capital Invested	Cash Flow	Financed By	% Equity	Tier
$200,000	$428.04/mo	IBC Policy Loan (Tier 1 Capital)	12.7497%	2

IG 55U LLC—55-Unit Multi-Family Rental (Tier 2—Investing)

☆ **Opportunity:** See 2024 Passive Income Report

☆ **Results:**

- The IG 55U LLC "middleman" entity was dissolved in 2025 and the owner's shares assumed, pro rata, by Rochester Holdings LLC. Without getting into the weeds, this was done to streamline accounting and save money on operating costs for tax purposes.
- Unfortunately, there was a fire in one of the four buildings that are part of this LLC, which significantly set back cash flow (distributions). Therefore, the expected return of about ~$1,200+/mo unfortunately turned into an average of $428.04/mo instead—due to several months with no distributions.
- Total distributions in 2025 = $5,136.52, imputing an anemic COC return of **2.57%**.
- Once the original $200K investment is returned (target: early 2026), COC return is projected to become infinite, as per the business plan.

Current COC Return: 2.57%

Projected COC Return within next 3–6 months: Infinite!

(following 100% return of capital)

#3 - Real Estate – Multi-Family Rentals in Multiple NH Towns				
Capital Invested	Cash Flow	Financed By	% Equity	Tier
$22,500	$210.59/mo	**IBC Policy Loan** (Tier 1 Capital)	7.22%	2

330 Central LLC—36-Unit Multi-Family Rental (Tier 2—Investing)

- ☆ **Opportunity:** See *2024 Passive Income Report*
- ☆ **Results:**
  - $3,527.07 paid out in 2025
  - My bullish 2024 COC projection was admittedly too sanguine. Actual COC return from this investment is calculated at 15.68%. I expect this to increase significantly in 2026.
  - Like other investments in this same camp, the COC return should become infinite once the business plan fully executes, and the properties are all refinanced (likely in the tail end of 2026)—returning 100% of capital back to the investor pool.

COC Return: 15.68%

Projected COC Return within 12 Months: Infinite!

#4 - Real Estate - BRRRR in Memphis, TN				
Capital Invested	**Cash Flow**	**Financed By**	**% Equity**	**Tier**
$29,939.33 (reduced to $0 post refi)	N/A (yet)	IBC Policy Loan (Tier 1 Capital)	33.33%	3

2100 Stovall—Fully-Managed BRRRR Rental (Tier 3—Investing)

☆ **Opportunity:** See *2024 Passive Income Report*

☆ **Results:**

- My partners and I worked with a local operator in the area to rehab this BRRRR property (Buy, Rehab, Rent, Refinance, Repeat). This rehab unfortunately took twice the time projected, but it did eventually get completed. We then secured a tenant paying $1,400/mo in rent. Following this, we refinanced the property at the anticipated revised valuation, allowing us to receive 100% of our initial investment to be returned to each of us! This, of course, put a mortgage in place. That mortgage is $652.56/mo + $108.44/mo (taxes and insurance) = $761.00. Thus, our cash flow is now $639.00/mo (or $7,668/yr).
- As we all got our initial principal returned, the COC return is effectively infinite (just the way I like it)! But even if I hadn't gotten a dime back with the refi, the COC return on this deal would still be respectable ($7,668 / 3 (I'm a one-third partner) / $29,939 = 8.54%). That said, I'll take infinite COC over 8.5% all day long. Using leverage is a powerful tool!

Cash Flow After Refinance: $639.00/mo

COC Return: Infinite!

#5 - Oil and Gas Investing – Managed Fund				
Capital Invested	**Cash Flow**	**Financed By**	**% Equity**	**Tier**
$250,000	$797.16/mo (dividend)	IBC Policy Loan (Tier 1 Capital)	100%	4

King Operating Partners II LP, Oil and Gas Fund (Tier 4—Speculating)

- ☆ **Opportunity:** See 2024 Passive Income Report
- ☆ **Results:** Total dividends paid in 2025 were $9,566.00. This imputes a 3.83% COC Return. This asset is both a cashFLOW play and a cashOUT play. Within the next two years, per the business plan, there should be efforts made to sell the oil field(s) to a big player and recoup investors as much as 3X their invested capital.

COC Return: 3.83%

Projected ROI by 2026/2027: 100%–300%

#6 - UPDATE - ATM Investing - Managed Fund (EXITED)				
Capital Invested	**Cash Flow**	**Financed By**	**% Equity**	**Tier**
$208,000	N/A	IBC Policy Loan (Tier 1 Capital)	100%	4

Prestige Fund D VI—ATM Fund (Tier 4—Speculating)

- ☆ **Opportunity:** See 2023 and 2024 Passive Income Report
- ☆ **Results:** This investment sadly did turn out to be a scam, as I feared going into 2025. While I got some of my money back before distributions completely dried up and the fund went belly-up, it was far from a full recoup. Daryl Heller is now facing criminal charges, and his company is in receivership. This reinforces the principle that *speculation* is risky. Tier 4 assets should only be purchased after careful and diligent research—and, even then, the operator must be vetted with extreme care.
- ☆ Many lessons were learned from this debacle, and I will take those lessons with me into my investing future!

#7 - UPDATE - STR Fund - Managed Fund				
Capital Invested	Cash Flow	Financed By	% Equity	Tier
$50,000	$695.25/yr	IBC Policy Loan (Tier 1 Capital)	100%	3

TVR 2 LLC, A-2 Tier, Techvestor STR Fund—TVR 2 LLC (Tier 3—Investing)

- ☆ **Opportunity:** See 2024 Passive Income Report
- ☆ **Results:** With the exception of the ATM (scam) described above, this STR fund has unfortunately been my worst performing asset in the last few years. Here are the listed distributions:
    - Jan 2025—$327.07
    - April 2025—$84.36
    - July 2025—$183.32
    - Oct 2025—$100.50
- ☆ *Anemic* is the word I would use to describe this. Frankly, I wish I had this capital back. I emailed and requested a way to exit the investment, and the fund manager, Sief Khafagi, said there were no options available. Do NOT invest in this fund (and I would argue any STR fund of a similar nature). Stay away.

COC Return 1.39%

#8 - UPDATE - Commercial Lobster Fishing Business (EXITED)				
Capital Invested	**Cash Flow**	**Financed By**	**% Equity**	**Tier**
$163,103	N/A	IBC Policy Loan (Tier 1 Capital)	25%	4

Fisher Lobster, LLC—Lobster Startup Business (Tier 4—Speculation)

☆ **Opportunity:** See 2024 Passive Income Report

☆ **Results:**

- In July 2025, after much prayerful consideration, my wife and I made the reluctant decision to exit this investment with a net loss. We sold the commercial fishing boat and the entire company to the operator we had running the business for the last couple of years.
- If you'd like the complete story behind this (including the governmental overreach and a litany of bureaucratic incompetence), I suggest purchasing the short book *A New Hampshire Lobsterman's Tale* by Derek Fisher, available here: **https://nhportauthority.com/**

#9 - UPDATE - Multi-Family Rental in Manchester, NH				
Capital Invested	Cash Flow	Financed By	% Equity	Tier
$150,000 (less $91,800 returned via refi) = $58,200.00	$1,297.86/mo	Debt @ 8.00%	50.00%	2

305 Cedar LLC—9-Unit Multi-Family Rental (Tier 2 - Investing)

- ☆ **Opportunity:** See 2023 and 2024 Passive Income Report
- ☆ **Results:**
    - In 2025 there were cash flows as follows:
        - $1,839.34 (Jan.)
        - $1,599.05 (Feb.)
        - $868.98 (Mar.)
        - $1,877.37 (Apr.)
        - $390.58 (May)
        - $805.34 (Jun.)
        - $1,704.39 (Jul)
        - $6,489.32 (Aug.-Dec.)
        - Total of $15,574.37 net cash flow in 2025
    - This imputes a COC Return (post-refi) of **26.76%**

COC Return: 26.76%

#10 - UPDATE - Lakehouse in Milton, NH (STR)				
Capital Invested	**Cash Flow**	**Financed By**	**% Equity**	**Tier**
$500,000 ($147,434.28 after refi)	$1,200/mo (each partner)	IBC Policy Loan (Tier 1 Capital)	33.33%	3

JASK Properties, LLC—STR Company (Tier 3—Investing)

- ☆ **Opportunity:** See *2024 Passive Income Report*
- ☆ Results:
    - As hoped, I was able to convince my two partners there was value in executing a strategic *cash-out refinance* to free up some capital for other ventures. By doing so, we were able to obtain a 30-year fixed 6.75% loan of $1,057,697.17. My one-third share of this was $352,565.72, which I promptly withdrew to invest in *Baxter Capital Group* multi-family asset purchases (see more info above and below). This reduced my total cash invested in JASK Properties LLC from $500,000 to $147,434.28.
    - In this same year, revenues unfortunately decreased year-over-year for the property by 28.95%. This is in line with the national trend of STRs (short-term rentals) nationwide seeing a dip in revenues between 25%-35%. Between 2024 and 2025, our property went from $141,940 in prime season revenues (Jan.-Sep. 2024) to $100,850 (Jan.-Sept. 2025), which imputes the nearly 30% drop described.
    - Taking on a mortgage obviously increased our loan interest costs for the business. We went from having zero mortgage interest to paying more than $60K in interest in the first year. This has obviously bitten into our profit margins. Adding insult to injury, our tax bill went up 46.62% year-over-year, and our insurance costs went up as well (including a bank-mandated requirement for us to get flood insurance for no reason whatsoever).
    - All in all, with expenses rising and revenues decreasing, we essentially broke even in 2025. So, while we did successfully

execute our cash-out refi as desired (freeing up significant capital for alternative investments), the resultant impact on our cash flow has caused a flattening effect, which I hope will improve in 2026.

COC Return: N/A

Projected COC in 2026: 9.76%

(assumes $14,400/yr in cash flow per partner)

#11 - Multi-Family Rentals in Raymond, Farmington and Manchester, NH				
Capital Invested	**Cash Flow**	**Financed By**	**% Equity**	**Tier**
$150,000	$1,321.85/mo	IBC Policy Loan (Tier 1 Capital)	10.454%	2

64Merrimack LLC—62-Unit Multi-Family Rental Portfolio (Tier 2—Investing)

- ☆ **Opportunity:** These multi-family deals where I can invest capital and get it all back within two years or less are like candy to me. They are extremely conservative investments, they create cash flow, they reduce my taxable income, and they are incredibly profitable. I grab them up with both fists!
- ☆ This case was a 62-unit multi-family real estate opportunity where several apartment buildings were purchased together in February 2025. Cash flow began flowing as early as May!
- ☆ **Results:**
  - In 2025 there were cash flows as follows:
    - $755.04 (May)
    - $1,307.33 (Jun.)
    - $1,656.94 (Jul.)
    - $1,568.10 (Aug.)
    - $5,287.41 (Sept.-Dec.) *[projected, based on average of preceding four months]*
    - $5,287.41 (Jan.-Apr.) *[imputed to make COC return calc possible]*
    - Total of $15,862.23 implied cash flow in 2025
- ☆ This imputes a COC Return of **10.57%**

COC Return: 10.57%

Projected COC Return within 24 Months: Infinite!

LOOKING INTO 2026 ...

Some goals going into 2026 include:

- ☆ Given the success of our Memphis TN BRRRR investment, potentially seek additional opportunities for executing the BRRRR strategy again there and elsewhere—but only assuming a strong operator is in place. A poor operator makes even the best business model fall flat on its face!
- ☆ Assist Tim Baxter with raising additional capital for extremely profitable multifamily real estate deals via the **Baxter Capital Multifamily Investment Fund**
    - (see: **www.BaxterCapital.net** for fund track record and business model)
- ☆ Focus more energy on growing my net worth via DEPTH not BREADTH (aka "deep not wide"). In other words, instead of investing capital and time on disparate ventures across many different asset classes or sectors, focus nearly exclusively on investing into more *multi-family real estate* deals. These conservative opportunities have consistently created the most cash flow, produced the best tax advantages (via using depreciation as a tax shield), and yielded the highest return. It's taken me many years to realize this, but the **best** asset class is not always the sexiest, but rather the one which is tried and true. I will be choosing *dependability* (Tier 2) over shiny objects (Tiers 3 and 4) going into 2026. To that end, as follows is a quick "cheat sheet" I created to help best focus my attention and focus when evaluating deals ...

What follows constitutes my "Buy Box" for 2026 and beyond. I have applied shading in the table to focus on the asset classes that check many, most, or all of my boxes. Specifically:

1. I want to see a relatively high and consistent **Cash on Cash Return** (COC %), for this is the "holy grail" for cash flow investors like me. If/when that metric will become INFINITE in a relatively short amount of time (meaning the asset continues to throw off passive income even after the initial capital invested has been fully returned), that makes the investment a homerun!
2. I want to almost exclusively invest in **Tier 2** asset classes, as they very often offer the *most consistent and highest returns* and are *simultaneously the least risky*.
3. I want the relative **Risk Level** of my investments to be *low*.
4. I want my **Effort** in these investments to be *low* (ideally none of my time required), making them truly passive.
5. I want **Unique Risks** to be limited almost exclusively to the *operator*, with only minor (or preferably no) market risk.
6. I will want **Depreciation** to work as a tax shield against my other passive income.
7. And lastly, to achieve #5 in abundance, I want to be able to take maximum advantage of the tax code and specifically 100% Bonus Depreciation if/whenever possible. To accomplish this, a **Cost Segregation Study** will ideally be possible to use on the asset to reduce my tax liability in the short (and long) term.

To represent these criteria across several passive income opportunities I'll be exploring in 2026, here are my evaluation metrics for multiple asset classes:

Asset Class	COC %	Tier	Risk Level	Effort	Unique Risks	Depreciation?	Cost Seg?
Multifamily Real Estate (Managed by PM + Refi'ed within 24 months or less) (i.e., "Baxter Capital Group Fund")	***6%–15%+ (infinite in y2!)***	2	Low	None	Manager/Operator	Yes	Yes
Multifamily Real Estate—Managed by PM	6%–12%	2	Low	None	Manager/Operator	Yes	Yes
Short-Term Rentals (STRs)—Managed by PM	8%–20%+	3	High	Med-High	Regulation, Operator	Yes	Yes
ATMs (Fund)	10%–12%	4	High	None	Obsolescence, Operator	Yes	Some
Oil and Gas Managed Funds	10%–15%+	4	High	None	Price Volatility, Fraud	Yes	Some
Self-Storage (Fund)	7%–12%	3	Med	None	Oversupply, Operator	Yes	Some
Car Washes (Fund)	8%–15%	3	Med	None	Equipment, Operator	Yes	Some
Mobile Home Parks	8%–15%	3	Med	High	Regulatory Risk (Lack of Inventory)	Yes	Yes
Private Lending (Uncollateralized)	12%–20%	3	Med-High	Med	Default Risk	No	No
Franchise Investing	8%–15%	3	Med	Med-High	Manager/Operator	No	No
Other Managed Funds (e.g., commercial RE)	5%–10%	2	Med-High	None	Fee Drag + Industry Risk(s), Operator	Maybe	No
Laundromats	7%–15%	3	Low-Med	High	Theft + Damage, City Regulation	Some	No
Billboards	6%–8%	3	Med	None	Zoning, Niche Market	Some	No
Farmland (REIT or Fund)	4%–8%	3	Low-Med	None	Weather, Crop Risk	No	No
Music or Book Royalties	5%–10%	2	High	None	Income Volatility	No	No
Dividend-Paying Stocks / Dividend-Paying ETFs	2%–6%	3–4	High	None	Market Risk	No	No
REITs (Public or Private)	4%–8%	3	Med	None	Market Risk	No	No

GLOSSARY

GLOSSARY

The Austrian Business Cycle Theory

- The Austrian Business Cycle Theory, as defined by Ludwig von Mises, posits that economic cycles are primarily driven by distortions in the interest rate caused by central bank interventions, particularly through artificially low interest rates. According to this theory, when a central bank lowers interest rates below the natural market rate, it encourages excessive borrowing and investment in long-term projects that are unsustainable in the long run.

- This leads to an economic boom characterized by overinvestment and malinvestment. However, once the market corrects itself and interest rates rise, these unsound investments are exposed, leading to a bust or recession. Mises argued that this boom-bust cycle is a consequence of monetary manipulation, and true economic stability can only be achieved through a free-market approach without central bank interference.

Collateralized Debt Obligation (CDO)

- A CDO (Collateralized Debt Obligation) is a type of financial instrument that pools together various loans, such as mortgages, bonds, or other forms of debt, and then divides this pool into tranches or layers that are sold to investors.

- Each tranche has a different level of risk and return, with higher-risk tranches offering higher potential returns. CDOs were widely used in the lead-up to the 2008 financial crisis, where their complexity and the underlying risk associated with simply packaging subprime mortgages into a new "now safe" derivative exponentially magnified the financial crisis.

Scarcity Mindset

☆ A scarcity mindset is a way of thinking that focuses on limitations and the fear of not having enough. People with a scarcity mindset often believe that resources—such as money, time, or opportunities—are finite and that when someone else gains, it comes at their own expense. This mindset can lead to anxiety, competition, and short-term thinking, as individuals may feel the need to hoard resources or miss out on potential opportunities because they are overly cautious.

Abundance Mindset

☆ An abundance mindset is the belief that there are enough resources and opportunities to go around for everyone. People with an abundance mindset focus on the possibilities and potential for growth, rather than on limitations. They tend to be more optimistic, collaborative, and open to taking risks, as they believe that success for others does not diminish their own chances for success. This mindset encourages long-term thinking, creativity, and a willingness to share and invest in others.

Infinite Banking Concept (IBC)

☆ The philosophy taught by Nelson Nash in his book "Becoming Your Own Banker." It deals with maximizing Cash Value (CV) in a series of whole life insurance policies in order to save money, achieve true uninterrupted compounding, maximize tax benefits, and have a pool of funds (your "bank") with which to invest in cash flow-producing assets.

Cash Value (CV)

- ☆ The total value available at any point to a practitioner of IBC. It is the liquid amount available in one's IBC "Bank."

Cash on Cash Return (COC Return)

- ☆ The annual cash flow of an investment (e.g., a rental property) divided by the total amount of cash used to purchase it.

Supply and Demand Curves

- ☆ This is one of the most important concepts to have a keen hold of in economics. It's relevant to understanding human behavior. When supply (the amount of something) goes up (and demand stays the same), the price of it will fall.

- ☆ Similarly, when the demand for something goes up (and supply stays the same), the price will go up. These two elements work best and satisfy the greatest number of people when they are not subject to artificial forces.

- ☆ Demand Curve:
  - **Definition:** The demand curve shows the relationship between the price of a good or service and the quantity that consumers are willing and able to purchase at different price levels.
  - **Shape:** The demand curve typically slopes downward from left to right, reflecting the law of demand: as the price of a good decreases, the quantity demanded increases, and vice versa.
  - **Determinants of Demand:** Factors that can shift the demand curve include changes in consumer preferences, income levels, the prices of related goods (substitutes and complements), inflation (the expansion of the supply of money or credit), and expectations about future prices.

- ☆ Supply Curve:
  - **Definition:** The supply curve illustrates the relationship between the price of a good or service and the quantity that producers are willing and able to sell at different price levels.
  - **Shape:** The supply curve generally slopes upward from left to right, reflecting the law of supply: as the price of a good increases, the quantity supplied increases, and vice versa.
  - **Determinants of Supply:** Factors that can shift the supply curve include changes in production costs, technology, the number of sellers in the market, and expectations about future prices.
- ☆ Equilibrium
  - **Intersection:** The point where the supply and demand curves intersect is called the equilibrium. At this point, the quantity of the good that consumers want to buy equals the quantity that producers want to sell, and the market price is established.
  - **Shifts:** If either the demand or supply curve shifts due to changes in external factors, the equilibrium price and quantity will also change.
- ☆ The supply and demand curves are fundamental concepts in economics, illustrating how prices and quantities are determined in competitive markets.
- ☆ As an example, if gasoline were mandated (let's say by the government) to cost $0.50/gallon, you can imagine how that would impact things. Consumers would purchase the current supply of gasoline or "hoard" it, leaving little or none for others.
- ☆ There would no longer be an incentive to produce/sell the product by suppliers. Those who needed it most (for example, emergency vehicles such as ambulances or fire trucks) would not be able to get it when needed.
- ☆ This would be an example of supply not being able to keep up with demand and creating a shortage. The market works best and achieves market equilibrium (i.e., when the greatest number of people can benefit) when prices are not set artificially. The price for gasoline best meets everyone's needs when supply and demand are equalized naturally (without "help" from the government or any external force).

The FDIC—Our "Safety Net Against Bank Failures"

- In 1933, during the Great Depression, the FDIC (Federal Deposit Insurance Corporation) was created, and one of its principal components is to guarantee money we put into the bank (checking and savings accounts).
- This is why we see "FDIC Insured" boldly proclaiming our assets are safe at all major and minor banking institutions. But here's the problem. There are 125.3 billion dollars in reserve (as of Q1 2024). That's a lot of money, sure. This means that many deposits are insured IF banks start to go belly up.
- However, 125.3B would only cover 0.25% of all total deposits in the U.S. In other words, only a quarter of a single percent is covered in the case of a major banking/financial catastrophe.
- So, our money is not really as "safe" as we think it is.

The Federal Reserve ("The FED")

"Without big banks, socialism would be impossible."
—Vladimir Lenin

- The Fed is the U.S. central bank. It was created December 23, 1913, by President Wilson. It directs much of the flow and creation of our nation's money supply, through use of the Treasury (which prints our paper money).
- Through its actions and policies men at the helm of the Fed can direct the interest rates of money in the U.S. via the purchase or sale of U.S. Treasuries.
- The Fed has never been audited, and, with the exception of meeting minutes, what happens at the central bank of the U.S. happens behind closed doors with little or no scrutiny or oversight.

> *"If the American people ever allow private banks to control the issue of their money, first by inflation and then by deflation, the banks and corporations that will grow up around them (around the banks), will deprive the people of their property until their children will wake up homeless on the continent their fathers conquered."*
> **–Thomas Jefferson**

- One of the biggest current problems with the Fed today is that it is creating money "out of thin air" by simply adding it to the ledgers of large banks. $100 bills aren't physically even printed. There currently are ~2.26 trillion physical dollars in circulation around the world. But there are ~83 trillion dollars on the books (deposited in banks). The difference is largely made up with the "made up" money the Fed gives to the banks and generates out of thin air.
- One can only wish the Constitution had addressed this evil more emphatically so that a central bank could NEVER have been permitted.
- Unfortunately, Hamilton knew that aristocratic business well, and as the first Secretary of the U.S. Treasury he charted the first U.S. central bank, the First Bank of the United States, against much opposition from Madison, Jefferson, and others. Jefferson killed it, though, as president and warned Americans never to attempt another.
- Of course, without a Constitutional prohibition on central banking, the bankers never stopped attempting to institute another private central bank. Today it has grown into an impenetrable leviathan–consuming the entire economy a little more, day by day.

Fractional Reserve Banking

- When we put money into a bank, that money is turned around and loaned out to others (i.e., as housing loans, corporate loans, etc). The bank maintains in its vault only a small fraction "in reserve." In other words, the bank only keeps a fraction of the money on hand and lends the rest of it. That may be 20%, 10%, or often as little as 3%!

- ☆ In this way, money can effectively be created out of thin air via a "multiplier effect." Here is how: the loaned money is lent as a note to a debtor and some portion of that money may then be put in ANOTHER bank; as such, the same system with the same reserve rate is in effect. Some is kept in reserves, but the remainder is lent out. Ergo, a single deposit of $1,000 can mathematically equate to over $100,000 in new money (assuming the reserve rate is 10%). That's theoretically 10x new money created from a single deposit.
- ☆ That's scary—but only if/when people want to pull their money out. Until then ... all is well. The deck of cards is undisturbed. But in this way, the fractional reserve banking system creates more money "out of thin air" each year than any other monetary system.

Fiat Money

- ☆ In 1971 Nixon took the U.S. off the gold standard. Before then our money (paper American bills) had an equivalent amount of gold for each dollar printed. It was kept in Fort Knox and elsewhere. But more importantly: we did not as drastically misuse the power enabling the Treasury to PRINT money on a whim as we do now unless the U.S. shored up a necessary amount of gold to back it.
- ☆ Now that we are off the gold standard, the only thing backing up our Benjamins is the steadfast word of Uncle Sam. This is called "fiat currency"—in other words, nothing concrete backs the paper money we use except the promise that it is worth what the U.S. government says it is worth. And this permits the system to carry through with practices (i.e., the unregulated printing and creation of money) which cause inflation to rise far faster than it might otherwise.

The "Bail-In"

- ☆ In 2008 the nature of a "bailout" was on everyone's lips. Whether you agreed with the administration's decisions made or not (hint: they were mostly all bad), the banking institutions were bailed-out by the American people after bad bets were made. In order to "save the economy" and "prevent utter collapse" we embraced the philosophy that some companies were "too big to fall." This is not news to anyone.
- ☆ Well, here's where the next fallout will come: the "bail-in." As a direct and knee-jerk reaction to public outrage and disgust (rightly so) the Dodd-Frank Act was signed into law. One of the elements put in place with this legislation was the near guarantee that banks will not be bailed out again (yay!).
- ☆ But guess what? A "bail-in" is therefore most likely to happen instead. This means that the money you deposit in a bank is not really yours; the moment it reaches the teller it is now legal property of the bank, and you are an '"UNSECURED creditor."
- ☆ As an unsecured creditor, you may be one of the last to be repaid should that bank go under. Why would the bank go under? Go back and see the notes about fractional reserve banking. In short, with the FDIC only able to cover a super small fraction of deposits (0.25%—that's a quarter of a single percent), individual depositors in banks may be screwed over in the end. This is not hypothetical; it's what happened in Cyprus and likely will happen here when the banking system collapses again.

Inflation

- ☆ Inflation happens in a country when the money supply increases at a rate causing goods and services to raise in price because the value of the money is not holding value.
- ☆ In the U.S., the Treasury is printing money with reckless abandon and the Fed is "creating" money at an unprecedented rate. Today (2025) the advertised rate of inflation is said to be ~4-5%/yr. But I don't believe that for a second!

- The REAL inflation rate is likely in the 13-15%/yr range (at best)—see the data on **ShadowStats**, which tracks the real rate of inflation before the **1995 Boskin Commission** played with the numbers.
- This means for money (my money, your money, etc) to actually not DECREASE in value just by sitting dormant, it must be invested or placed in an account that makes 15%+ just to keep pace with inflation.
- That is nearly impossible to do in America. So, as a result, investors and retirees alike are flocking to riskier and riskier investments just to try to meet and beat inflation. They chase yield!

Postmodernism

- Postmodernism emerged as a reaction to the principles of modernism and the Enlightenment's emphasis on objective truth, progress, and rationality.
- It is a deconstructive framework, unfortunately with little to no emphasis on reconstruction.
- Originating in the mid-20th century, it draws from various intellectual movements, including structuralism, deconstruction, and critiques of grand narratives. Postmodernist philosophy argues that reality and truth are not objective but are constructed through language, cultural contexts, and power structures.
- This wild perspective holds that since knowledge and meaning are shaped by individual and collective interpretations rather than universal truths, people can create their own realities and challenge established facts.
- Consequently, postmodernism often emphasizes relativism and skepticism about absolute knowledge, leading to a view that multiple, sometimes conflicting, interpretations can coexist.

"Formal education will make you a living; self-education will make you a fortune."

—Jim Rohn

INDEX

D

E

F

G

H

I

J

K

L

M

N

O

P

Q

U

V

W

Y

About the

AUTHOR

Sean Dempsey

Sean Dempsey is a 2007 graduate of the University of Vermont where he received his degree in Business Administration; he later went on to receive his MBA at the University of New Hampshire.

Sean is a writer, a poet, a husband, and a father.

He is also a real estate investor, entrepreneur, and business owner—having founded nine successful New Hampshire-based companies.

Sean is a student of Robert Kiyosaki as well as an avid practitioner of Nelson Nash's Infinite Banking Concept (IBC).

This book was a passion project and a distillation of Sean's body of investment knowledge accumulated to date.

Sean's personal website can be found at www.seandempsey.com.

About the ILLUSTRATOR

Jason D. McIntosh is an SCBWI award-winning illustrator from New Hampshire whose artistic career sprouted in the fourth grade while marketing artwork to friends. Since then, he has championed thousands of design projects worldwide. When not writing or doodling, he is often found adventuring through the woods with his wife and six children or meandering through the lands of Middle Earth, Narnia, Redwall Abbey, and the like.

His current mission: Create thoughtful illustrations and stories that inspire. You can view more of his work at: **www.jasondmcintosh.com**